COOKING
FOR
CHRISTMAS

COOKING FOR CHRISTMAS

Rosemary Wadey

Contents

First published in 1984 by Octopus Books Limited
59 Grosvenor Street, London W1

Fourth impression, 1985

© 1984 Hennerwood Publications Limited

ISBN 0 86273 161 5

Printed in Hong Kong

INTRODUCTION

However it is celebrated, Christmas is always Christmas – a time of gaiety and celebration and, most important, of eating and drinking. It is the one time in the year when all scruples about diet or expense can be forgotten in a glorious bout of self-indulgence.

This book is aimed at covering every aspect of Christmas food, from the most traditional Christmas dinner to the simple supper or drinks party snack. We have also tried to provide food for thought for those households looking for new ideas. Whatever your preference, this book is aimed at easing the load on the cook, too often left to slave away on her own, and to provide enough inspiration to carry you sailing through with the least effort and most effect.

COOKING AHEAD

The simplest way to beat the problem of the Christmas workload is to cook ahead – even easier if you have a freezer. The well-prepared cook with a carefully mapped-out calendar has a tremendous advantage over those who are thrown into a last-minute panic.

This book starts several months ahead with the early preparation of the Christmas puddings, cakes and mincemeat. All these improve with long maturing, and cooking them in advance will help to ease the pressure of those last hectic few days immensely. This chapter also covers the preparation of all the icing and marzipan decorations, a fiddly, time-consuming last-minute task. This job is an ideal one to get out of the way early, as the decorations will store for several months. Mince-pies, flans, pastries and other useful fill-ins for the odd meals that crop up between feasting can also be made in advance and stored in the freezer. In all cases, storage and thawing times are given. And for the incurable last-minute cook, a word of comfort; puddings, mincemeat and cakes, although the better for storage, can quite successfully be made at the eleventh hour with no problems.

12 DAYS OF CHRISTMAS

Traditionally, Christmas is spread over 12 days, beginning on Christmas Eve and ending on January 6th (Twelfth Night), the day decorations must be taken down or bad luck will befall the house. In the middle of this period is the New Year, always a good excuse for a party. Whether you break for one or two days or are lucky enough to have an extended holiday covering the whole period, food (and drink) is likely to play a large part in your celebrations. Planning your menus day by day can be a tremendous help, as much of the food will have to be bought in advance. The suggestions for menus for the 12 days are designed to cover every situation. They provide ideas for starters, main courses, vegetable accompaniments and desserts for every occasion.

CHRISTMAS LEFTOVERS

The problem of cold turkey leftovers is almost proverbial – many cooks cringe at the very thought of it. Here we give some recipes to transform your leftovers quickly and easily into delicious meals.

ALTERNATIVE CHRISTMAS

With the advent of more adventurous eating habits, and the current cheapness of turkey making it less of a treat, turkey is no longer the only possible Christmas choice, as fixed and unchanging as the date itself. Although it will probably remain the favourite for the majority, we have included alternatives for those who like to ring the changes. Among these are types of game, including venison, partridge and wild duck, all very rich in flavour, as well as a royal rib of roast beef, England's traditional meat for Christmas before America introduced the turkey. As well, we have considered those who have a special reason for not eating turkey – calorie-counted food for slimmers, vegetarian recipes, and a mouthwatering salmon en croûte for those who prefer fish.

CAKES

In spite of having eaten an enormous meal, everyone is always ready for tea. This is often the children's favourite meal and as Christmas is especially for children, it should not be neglected. Traditionally, a rich fruit cake with marzipan and icing is served – and we give details for several designs. For those who don't like fruit cake, recipes for richly frosted chocolate and coffee favourites are included – plain cakes special enough to replace the traditional one. There is also a wide selection for those who find the heavy traditional icing a little oversweet – Dundee and glacé cherry cakes as well as the plainer madeira (which can also be iced).

CHRISTMAS ABROAD

Finally, Christmas is celebrated in its own way in many countries all over the world. Lots of them share our traditional food but many others don't, and the final chapter includes some of these foreign favourites for the Christmas holiday. Add them to your repertoire for an exciting change: there are some delicious discoveries to be made. The Greek New Year's cake has a marvellous flavour and melting texture; Christmas pudding from New Zealand has to be tried both on its own and in its very special Maori version, while the Christmas tree cookies will soon disappear from the tree.

Christmas is a time of joy and families, giving and receiving, of friendliness and fun, but it can also mean a lot of hard work and last-minute panic when time or ideas run thin. We hope this book will give you plenty of both – ideas to enliven your Christmas with variations on old favourites or interesting new alternatives, and time to spend Christmas as you would like to, free from worry.

Merry Christmas!

Cooking Ahead

Granny's Christmas puddings

Serves 8 from large pudding bowl or 4 from small pudding bowl	1 cooking apple, peeled, cored and grated
225 g (8 oz) sultanas	225 g (8 oz) shredded suet
225 g (8 oz) currants	½ teaspoon mixed spice
225 g (8 oz) seedless raisins	pinch of ground or grated nutmeg
225 g (8 oz) stoned raisins, chopped	½ teaspoon ground cinnamon
50 g (2 oz) cut mixed peel	225 g (8 oz) demerara sugar
100 g (4 oz) glacé cherries, chopped	grated rind and juice of 1 large lemon
100 g (4 oz) blanched almonds, chopped	grated rind and juice of 1 orange
100 g (4 oz) ground almonds	225 g (8 oz) golden syrup
225 g (8 oz) fresh breadcrumbs, brown or white	4 eggs, beaten
	4 tablespoons brandy
	150 ml (¼ pint) brown ale
2 carrots, scraped and grated	lard, for greasing basins

Preparation time: *about 30 minutes, plus cooling overnight*
Cooking time: *6–8 hours plus 3–4 hours before serving, or 3 hours in a pressure cooker and 1 hour before serving*

This recipe gives a very moist pudding which keeps well for up to 2 years. Originally the puddings were made during the last weekend of November – giving everyone a stir on 'Stir Sunday' – to be eaten the following year. Nowadays it is more usual to make the puddings 3–6 months in advance – although you can of course make them at the last minute if you have to.

1. Place all the ingredients in a large mixing bowl, stirring well to mix.
2. Grease 3 × 1.2 litre (2 pint) pudding basins or 6 × 600 ml (1 pint) basins well with lard. Fill each basin just over three-quarters full, then cover with greased greaseproof paper and foil or a pudding cloth. Tie securely with string.
3. Place each pudding in a saucepan and pour in boiling water to come halfway up the sides. Boil for 6–8 hours depending on size. Top up with more boiling water as necessary. Remove the puddings from the pans and leave overnight to cool completely.
4. Remove the coverings and cover again with fresh greased greaseproof paper and foil or a pudding cloth. Store in a cool, dry place away from direct sunlight, a dark larder would do.
5. To serve: reboil for 3–4 hours, depending on size, then turn out on to a warm dish and serve with brandy butter and/or cream and sugar. To ignite the pudding: warm 3–4 tablespoons brandy, pour over the pudding and set alight carefully. If decorating with a piece of holly on top, wrap the stem in a small piece of foil.

To cook the puddings in a pressure cooker
1. Prepare and cover as above. Stand the basin on the rack in the pan and add 1.5–1.75 litres (2½–3 pints) water. Follow manufacturer's instructions. Put on the weights, bring to pressure and cook for the required time allowing 3 hours at high for large puddings or 2¼ hours for small ones. Reduce the pressure slowly, remove the pudding and leave to cool overnight. Re-cover as above. Before serving, pressure-cook at high pressure for 1 hour for the large pudding or 45 minutes for the small one.

Christmas puddings

Makes 1 large and 1 small pudding	1 small apple, peeled, cored and grated
100 g (4 oz) self-raising flour	grated rind and juice of 1 small orange
175 g (6 oz) fresh white breadcrumbs	½ teaspoon mixed spice
175 g (6 oz) currants	¼ teaspoon ground or grated nutmeg
175 g (6 oz) sultanas	½ teaspoon salt
100 g (4 oz) stoned dates, chopped	3 eggs
225 g (8 oz) stoned raisins	4 tablespoons brown ale or cider
175 g (6 oz) shredded suet	225 g (8 oz) dark soft brown sugar
50 g (2 oz) cut mixed peel	
50 g (2 oz) blanched almonds, chopped	lard, for greasing basins

Preparation time: *about 30 minutes*
Cooking time: *6–8 hours plus 3–4 hours before serving or 3 hours in a pressure cooker and 1 hour before serving*

1. Thoroughly combine all the ingredients in a large mixing basin. Turn into a well greased 1.2 litre (2 pint) and a 600 ml (1 pint) basin and cover as for Granny's Christmas puddings.
2. Either boil or cook in the pressure cooker as for Granny's Christmas puddings and store in the same way.

Granny's Christmas puddings

Mincemeat

Makes about 3 kg (7 lb)

450 g (1 lb) currants, chopped

450 g (1 lb) sultanas, chopped

450 g (1 lb) seedless raisins, chopped

450 g (1 lb) cut mixed peel

100 g (4 oz) blanched almonds, finely chopped

450 g (1 lb) cooking apples, peeled, cored and coarsely grated

450 g (1 lb) dark soft brown sugar

225 g (8 oz) shredded suet, chopped

1 teaspoon ground or grated nutmeg

1 teaspoon ground cinnamon

1 teaspoon mixed spice

grated rind of 2 lemons

juice of 1 lemon

2–4 tablespoons brandy

Preparation time: *20–30 minutes, plus standing*

1. Put the currants, sultanas, raisins, mixed peel and almonds into a large mixing bowl. Add the apple, sugar, suet, spices and lemon rind and juice. Stir thoroughly.
2. Cover the bowl with cling film and leave for 2 days.
3. Stir the mincemeat again very thoroughly, draining off any excess liquid. Stir in the brandy. Pack the mincemeat into clean jars, cover as for jam, label and store in a cool, dry place for at least 2 weeks before use.

Freezer mincemeat

Makes approx. 1.75 kg (4 lb)

675–900 g (1½–2 lb) cooking apples, peeled, cored and finely chopped

225 g (8 oz) currants, chopped

225 g (8 oz) sultanas, chopped

225 g (8 oz) seedless raisins, chopped

225 g (8 oz) cut mixed peel

75 g (3 oz) blanched almonds, chopped

450 g (1 lb) soft dark brown sugar

100 g (4 oz) shredded suet, chopped

1 teaspoon ground nutmeg

1 teaspoon ground cinnamon

grated rind of 1 orange

grated rind and juice of 1 lemon

Preparation time: *about 30 minutes*
Cooking time: *about 5 minutes*

1. Blanch the apples in boiling water for 30 seconds, then drain very thoroughly in a colander and cool.
2. Combine the currants, sultanas and raisins with the mixed peel in a large mixing bowl. Stir in the almonds, sugar, suet and spices. Add the drained apple, orange and lemon rind and lemon juice and stir thoroughly to mix.
3. Freeze in plastic containers or small freezer polythene bags in 225 g (8 oz) quantities, for up to 4 months. Thaw overnight in the refrigerator before using.

Mincemeat jalousie

Serves 6–8

225 g (8 oz) puff pastry, made using 225 g (8 oz) plain flour (page 16)

450 g (1 lb) mincemeat or freezer mincemeat (page 10)

50 g (2 oz) glacé cherries, chopped

25 g (1 oz) blanched almonds, finely chopped

2 tablespoons brandy or rum

1 egg white, beaten or a little milk, to glaze

little caster sugar, to dredge

Preparation time: *20–25 minutes*
Cooking time: *25–30 minutes*
Oven: *220°C, 425°F, Gas Mark 7*

1. Roll out the pastry on a lightly floured board or work surface and trim to a 30 cm (12 inch) square. Cut in half and place one piece on a lightly greased baking sheet.
2. Roll out the second piece of pastry to a 33 × 20 cm (13 × 8 inch) rectangle, then fold in half lengthways. Using a sharp knife, cut into the fold at 1 cm (½ inch) intervals to within 2.5 cm (1 inch) of the edges and ends.
3. Thoroughly combine the mincemeat, cherries, almonds and brandy. Spread the mixture over the pastry on the baking sheet to within 2.5 cm (1 inch) of the edges.
4. Brush the edges of the pastry with water and cover with the pastry for the lid, carefully unfolding it to cover the filling completely, and making sure the edges fit together neatly.
5. Press the pastry edges together firmly to seal, then flake the edges all around with a sharp knife and scallop the rim with the fingers and the back of the knife. ☐F
6. Brush the top all over with egg white and dredge lightly but evenly with sugar. Bake just below the centre of a preheated hot oven for 25–30 minutes until the pastry is well risen and golden brown. ☐F Serve hot or cold, cut into slices, with ice cream or cream.

☐F Can be frozen cooked or uncooked, wrapped in foil or cling film. If frozen cooked, it should be refreshed for a few minutes in the oven after thawing for 6–8 hours.

Mincemeat jalousie

Mince pies

Makes 16–18

225 g (8 oz) Special shortcrust pastry (page 18)

450 g (1 lb) mincemeat or freezer mincemeat (page 10)

1 egg white, beaten, or a little milk, to glaze

caster sugar, to dredge

Preparation time: *30 minutes, plus cooling*
Cooking time: *20 minutes*
Oven: *200°C, 400°F, Gas Mark 6*

1. Roll out the pastry and with a fluted 7.5 cm (3 inch) pastry cutter cut out 16–18 rounds. Cut out 16–18 slightly smaller rounds for the lids.

2. Fit the large rounds into greased patty tins and spoon about 2 teaspoons mincemeat into each one. Dampen the edges of the lids and press down lightly to seal. **F**

3. Brush the tops of the mince pies with egg white and dredge lightly with sugar. Make a small hole in the top of each mince pie and bake in a fairly hot oven for about 20 minutes. Leave to cool slightly in the tins, then carefully transfer to a wire tray to cool completely.

F Open-freeze in patty tins then remove and pack in rigid containers. To serve, replace in patty tins and bake from frozen as directed.

Christmas cake

225 g (8 oz) butter or margarine

225 g (8 oz) dark soft brown sugar

4 eggs

225 g (8 oz) plain flour, sifted

1 teaspoon mixed spice

½ teaspoon ground cinnamon

¼ teaspoon ground mace or nutmeg

2 tablespoons black treacle

1 tablespoon lemon or orange juice

225 g (8 oz) seedless raisins

350 g (12 oz) currants

225 g (8 oz) sultanas

100 g (4 oz) cut mixed peel

50 g (2 oz) blanched almonds, chopped

75 g (3 oz) glacé cherries, quartered, washed and dried

grated rind of 1 lemon

grated rind of 1 small orange

3–4 tablespoons brandy

Preparation time: *40 minutes, plus cooling overnight*
Cooking time: *about 3 ½ hours*
Oven: *150°C, 300°F, Gas Mark 2*

1. Grease and line a 20 cm (8 inch) round or 18 cm (7 inch) square deep cake tin with greased greaseproof paper.

2. In a large mixing bowl cream the butter and sugar until very light and fluffy. Beat in the eggs one at a time, folding in a tablespoon of flour after each addition.

3. Sift the remaining flour with the spices and fold into the creamed mixture, using a large metal spoon. Then stir in the treacle and fruit juice.

4. Combine the raisins, currants, sultanas, mixed peel, almonds, cherries and lemon and orange rind. Add to the cake mixture and stir until evenly blended, then turn into the prepared tin. Smooth the surface, make a small hollow in the centre and tie a treble thickness of brown paper around the outside of the tin.

5. Bake in a preheated cool oven for about 3¼–3½ hours or until a warmed fine skewer inserted into the centre of the cake comes out clean.

6. Leave the cake in the tin overnight to cool completely. Prick the surface all over with a fine skewer, then pour over the brandy and allow to soak in. Remove the cake from the tin, wrap securely in foil and store in a cool, dry place. **F**

F Wrap the cake securely in foil and freeze for up to 6 months. Thaw overnight at room temperature.

For these Christmas cakes, please follow the recipe instructions (rather than the photograph opposite) by using brown paper and *not* newspaper.

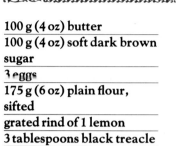

Christmas cake with dates

100 g (4 oz) butter

100 g (4 oz) soft dark brown sugar

3 eggs

175 g (6 oz) plain flour, sifted

grated rind of 1 lemon

3 tablespoons black treacle

pinch of ground cloves

pinch of ground or grated nutmeg

¼ teaspoon ground cinnamon

½ teaspoon mixed spice

175 g (6 oz) currants

175 g (6 oz) sultanas

100 g (4 oz) seedless raisins

50 g (2 oz) stoned dates, finely chopped

50 g (2 oz) cut mixed peel

50 g (2 oz) glacé cherries, quartered, washed and dried

2 tablespoons lemon juice

2 tablespoons brandy or rum

Preparation time: *30 minutes*
Cooking time: *2½–3 hours*
Oven: *160°C, 325°F, Gas Mark 3*

1. Grease an 18 cm (7 inch) deep round cake tin and line with greased greaseproof paper.

2. In a large mixing bowl cream the butter and sugar until very light and fluffy. Beat in the eggs one at a time, folding in a tablespoon of flour after each addition, then beat in the lemon rind and treacle.

3. Sift the remaining flour with the spices and fold into the mixture, using a large metal spoon.

4. Combine the currants, sultanas, raisins, dates, mixed peel and cherries and add to the mixture. Stir in the lemon juice and brandy, to give a soft dropping consistency.

5. Turn the mixture into the prepared tin, smooth the surface and make a slight hollow in the centre. Tie a treble thickness of brown paper around the outside of the tin.

6. Bake in a preheated moderate oven for about 3 hours or until a warmed fine skewer inserted into the centre of the cake comes out clean.

7. Leave the cake in the tin overnight to cool completely, then wrap in foil to store. If the cake is to be kept longer than 4 weeks, pierce the top of the cake with a skewer and sprinkle with 3 tablepoons brandy or rum before wrapping in foil.

LEFT: Christmas cake RIGHT: Christmas cake with dates

Christmas cake decorations

All these decorations can be made 3–8 weeks in advance. They must be made at least a week in advance, especially if using deeply coloured marzipan, for if this is put on to white icing before either is quite dry the colour may seep on to the icing and spoil the effect. Use either your own marzipan or icings (page 70) or, if time is short, commercial marzipan or fondant icing for moulding.

Use a good food colouring for working into the marzipan or icing (special pastes and powders are available for really deep colours). Experiment with mixing the colours too. Knead into marzipan or fondant icing until evenly coloured and no longer streaky. Add to royal icing with a skewer dipped into the colouring then just touched on to the icing, to avoid over-colouring. White icings are the easiest to colour, and a commercial almost white marzipan is available which is also ideal for colouring. Extra colour may be painted on to marzipan and icing flowers and leaves using liquid food colourings and a very fine paint brush. N.B. Marzipan does not freeze well because of its very high fat content.

Marzipan

Rolling out marzipan between two sheets of polythene or non-stick silicone paper makes the job easier and less sticky, giving a more even result. Once they are completely dry the marzipan decorations can be stored in airtight containers layered up with greaseproof, waxed or non-stick paper. If they are stored in this way, marzipan decorations will keep for up to 2 months.

Holly Leaves and Berries

Make a dark green marzipan by moulding green, blue and a touch of brown food colouring into the marzipan. Roll out thinly and cut into rectangles about 2.5–4 cm (1–1½ inches) long and 2 cm (¾ inch) wide. Using a tiny round aspic or petits fours cutter, or the base of a piping nozzle, make leaves by taking cuts out of the edges of the marzipan rectangles. Mark a vein down the centre of each one with a sharp knife and leave to dry on non-stick silicone paper, or lay over a lightly greased wooden spoon handle for curved leaves. For the berries, tint a small piece of marzipan deep red and shape into tiny balls, rolling them between the palms of the hands. Leave to dry completely (at least 24 hours).

Christmas Trees

Draw a pattern for a simple Christmas tree to the size required on a piece of greaseproof paper. Using the pattern as a guide, cut out Christmas trees from thinly rolled out green marzipan and leave to dry completely. A tub may be made from red marzipan. For decorations apply tiny silver or coloured balls to the tips of the branches with a dab of icing.

Ivy Leaves and Mistletoe

Draw patterns in several sizes for ivy leaves and mistletoe leaves on a piece of greaseproof paper. Use a mid-green marzipan and an even paler green for the mistletoe. Cut out the ivy leaves from thinly rolled out mid-green marzipan and the mistletoe leaves from pale green marzipan. Mark the veins with a sharp knife and leave to dry completely. Mistletoe berries, which are larger than holly berries, may be made from white marzipan.

Moulded flowers

Use marzipan or commercial fondant icing (now widely available) and colour it as you wish, kneading it in.

Roses

Roll out the marzipan or fondant icing very thinly and for each flower cut out 2 × 1 cm (½ inch) circles. Hold the circles at one side and with the fingers of the other hand carefully press out the rest of the circle until very thin and almost transparent. Roll the first one up for the centre of the rose and wrap the second petal around it, fairly tightly at the base but leaving it loose at the top to show the centre. (If using fondant icing, you may need a dab of water to make the petals stick firmly.) Continue to make 3 or 4 more petals in the same way, each a fraction larger than the previous one, and attach in the same way, keeping a good curve so that the result really looks like a rose and not a cabbage. For a small rose 4 petals are sufficient, but a larger one may need 7 or 8. Leave to dry on non-stick silicone paper or on upturned egg boxes for up to a week before storing carefully between layers of non-stick silicone or waxed paper in an airtight container.

Christmas Roses

Make these by moulding the marzipan or fondant icing to give 5 petals, each with a rounded point and slightly upturned edge. Assemble the rose as described above and fill the centre with minute yellow balls of marzipan or fondant icing, or pipe in dots of yellow royal icing for the stamens. Leave to dry completely in a cool place before storing them in an airtight container.

Piped royal icing flowers

To make icing flowers you need an icing nail or cork impaled on a small skewer, a quantity of non-stick silicone paper cut into 4 cm (1½ inch) squares and a paper or plastic piping bag fitted with a medium petal nozzle. Half fill the icing bag with royal icing (page 70).

Roses

Attach a square of paper to the icing nail with a dab of icing. Hold the piping bag with the thin edge of the petal nozzle upwards. Squeezing gently and evenly and twisting the nail at the same time, pipe a tight coil for the centre of the rose. Continue to add 5 or 6 petals, one at a time, piping the icing and twisting at the same time but taking each petal only about three-quarters of the way around the flower. Begin in a different part of the flower each time to keep the shape even, and hold the base of the nozzle in towards the centre of the flower to prevent the rose expanding at the base and the top and losing its shape. The petals can be kept tight to form a rosebud or more open for full-blown flowers. Leave to dry on the paper for at least 24 hours before removing from the paper, and when dry store in an airtight container. If the icing roses are at all damp they will go mouldy.

Roses can be made in any colour you like.

Christmas Roses

This is a flat flower, which should be made with white icing. Begin with the thick edge of the petal nozzle to the centre. Keep the nozzle flat and form each petal separately. Gently squeeze out the icing. Take the tip outwards to a rounded point, keeping the petals slightly tilted upwards at the edges like a 'tea-rose', then bring it back towards the centre, twisting it slightly and gradually releasing the pressure. This gives a single petal. Make 4 more in the same way to give an even flower, making each one slightly underlap its neighbour by placing the nozzle just under the previous petal as you begin to pipe. Leave to dry completely, then pipe pale to deeper yellow icing dots in the centre for the stamens. Leave to dry again completely.

Pastries to freeze

Shortcrust

225 g (8 oz) plain flour
pinch of salt
50 g (2 oz) lard
50 g (2 oz) butter or block
margarine
cold water, to mix

1. Sift the flour and salt into a mixing bowl. Rub in the lard and butter, using the fingertips, until the mixture resembles fine breadcrumbs.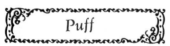
2. Add enough water to mix to a pliable dough, using a round-bladed knife. Knead lightly.
3. Wrap the dough in a polythene freezer bag or foil and freeze for up to 6 months. Thaw for 2–3 hours at room temperature before using and bake in a hot oven (220°C, 425°F, Gas Mark 7).

A The rubbed-in dry mixture can be stored in an air-tight container for up to 3 weeks.

Puff

450 g (1 lb) plain flour
1 teaspoon salt
450 g (1 lb) butter, firm but
not too hard
approx 300 ml (½ pint) iced
water
squeeze of lemon juice

Preparation time: *about 40 minutes, plus chilling time*

1. Sift the flour and salt into a mixing bowl. Rub 75 g (3 oz) of the butter into the flour, using the fingertips. Add enough iced water and lemon juice to mix to a fairly soft dough, using a round-bladed knife. Knead lightly.
2. Roll out the pastry on a lightly floured board or work surface to a 30 cm (12 inch) square.
3. Soften the remaining butter a little and form into an oblong block; place on one half of the pastry square. Fold the pastry over to enclose the butter and seal the pastry edges with the rolling pin. 'Rib' the pastry by pressing the rolling pin across it at regular intervals.
4. Turn the pastry so that the fold is to the right and roll out to a rectangle three times as long as it is wide. Fold the bottom third upwards and the top third downwards. Seal the edges with the rolling pin, 'rib' and place in a polythene bag. Chill in the refrigerator for 30 minutes.
5. Repeat the rolling, folding and chilling process 5 times, giving the pastry a quarter turn each time so that the fold is always on the right.
6. Chill the pastry for at least 1 hour, preferably overnight, before use. Alternatively cut in half, wrap in a freezer polythene bag or foil and freeze for up to 3 months. Thaw for 2–3 hours at room temperature before using and bake in a hot to very hot oven (220–230°C, 425–450°F, Gas Mark 7–8).

Stuffings

Pâté and chestnut stuffing

To stuff a 4.5–7.25 kg
(10–16 lb) turkey
1 tablespoon vegetable oil
1 onion, peeled and finely
chopped
1 clove garlic, crushed
(optional)
1–2 tablespoons chopped
fresh parsley
½ teaspoon dried thyme
salt
freshly ground black
pepper
100 g (4 oz) smooth liver
pâté
175 g (6 oz) whole peeled
cooked chestnuts, or
unsweetened chestnut
purée
100 g (4 oz) fresh white
breadcrumbs
1 egg, beaten
a little lemon juice

Preparation time: *about 15 minutes*

1. Heat the oil in a frying pan, add the onion and garlic, if using, and fry over a gentle heat for about 5 minutes until soft and lightly coloured. Remove from the heat and turn into a bowl. Mix in the parsley and thyme and season well with salt and pepper.

2. Mash the pâté with the chestnuts and add to the onion mixture with the breadcrumbs. Stir well to mix, then add the egg and enough lemon juice to bind to a paste which is not too stiff.

3. The stuffing may be frozen for up to 4 weeks. Thaw completely before using (about 4–6 hours).

Preparing turkey stuffings

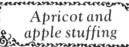

Apricot and apple stuffing

To stuff a 4.5–7.25 kg (10–16 lb) turkey	1 small onion, peeled and finely chopped
50 g (2 oz) dried apricots, finely chopped	2 celery sticks, finely chopped
a little boiling water	1 cooking apple, peeled, cored and finely chopped
1 tablespoon vegetable oil	salt
50 g (2 oz) streaky bacon rashers, rinded, boned and chopped	freshly ground black pepper
	75 g (3 oz) fresh white breadcrumbs
	1 egg yolk

Preparation time: *about 30 minutes, plus soaking*

1. Put the apricots in a bowl, cover with boiling water and leave to soak for 2–3 hours. Drain well.

2. Heat the oil in a frying pan, add the bacon and fry over a moderate heat, stirring from time to time, until browned. Using a slotted spoon, remove the bacon and add to the apricots. Add the onion and celery to the pan and fry for 2–3 minutes. Add the apple and fry for 2–3 further minutes.

3. Add the onion and apple mixture to the apricots with the breadcrumbs. Season well with salt and pepper. Stir in the egg yolk to bind to a paste which is not too stiff. Add a little lemon juice if necessary. Freeze as for the Pâté and chestnut stuffing.

Walnut, orange and coriander

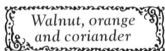

To stuff a 4.5–7.25 kg (10–16 lb) turkey	50 g (2 oz) shelled walnuts, finely chopped
25 g (1 oz) butter or margarine	50–75 g (2–3 oz) seedless raisins, roughly chopped
1 onion, peeled and chopped	150 g (5 oz) fresh white breadcrumbs
2 teaspoons ground coriander	salt
	freshly ground black pepper
grated rind of 1 orange	1 egg, beaten
	1–2 tablespoons fresh orange juice
	2 tablespoons chopped fresh parsley

Preparation time: *15 minutes*

1. Melt the butter in a frying pan, add the onion and fry over a gentle heat for about 10 minutes until soft and golden brown. Remove from the heat and turn into a bowl. Add the coriander, orange rind, walnuts, raisins and breadcrumbs and season well with salt and pepper. Stir well to mix.

2. Add the egg and enough orange juice to bind to a paste which is not too stiff. Freeze as for the Pâté and chestnut stuffing.

Pissaladière

Serves 6–8
150 g (6 oz) shortcrust pastry made with 150 g (6 oz) plain flour (page 16)
3 tablespoons vegetable oil
350 g (12 oz) onions, peeled and thinly sliced
2–3 cloves garlic, crushed
salt
freshly ground black pepper
2 × 425 g (15 oz) cans peeled tomatoes
50 g (2 oz) mature Cheddar cheese, finely grated
1 can anchovy fillets in oil, drained and halved lengthways
black olives, to garnish

Preparation time: *30 minutes*
Cooking time: *about 45 minutes*
Oven: *220°C, 425°F, Gas Mark 7*
then: *190°C, 375°F, Gas Mark 5*

1. Roll out the pastry on a lightly floured board or work surface and use to line a 23–25 cm (9–10 inch) flan tin or dish. Bake blind in a preheated hot oven for 20 minutes, then remove and reduce the oven temperature.
2. Heat the oil in a frying pan, add the onions and garlic and fry over a gentle heat for about 5 minutes until soft and lightly coloured. Remove from the heat and allow to cool slightly.
3. Spoon the onions into the pastry case, to cover the base evenly. Season with salt and pepper.
4. Drain the tomatoes and chop roughly (reserve the juice for another use). Spoon the tomatoes over the onions and sprinkle with the cheese. Arrange the anchovy fillets on top in a lattice pattern, and add the olives.
5. Bake in a preheated moderate oven for about 20 minutes until the pastry is cooked and the filling piping hot.
6. Allow to cool completely. Wrap in foil or cling film and store carefully in the freezer. Thaw for 8–12 hours. Serve hot or cold.

Choux buns

Makes 20–24
100 g (4 oz) butter
300 ml (½ pint) water
125 g (5 oz) plain flour
pinch of salt
4 eggs, beaten

Preparation time: *20 minutes*
Cooking time: *about 30 minutes*
Oven: *220°C, 425°F, Gas Mark 7*

These choux buns can be split and filled with a savoury mixture to serve as a snack or at a cocktail party, either hot or cold; or to use as profiteroles or in a variety of other desserts, with a cream-based filling (page 34).

1. Grease 2 or 3 baking sheets. Melt the butter in a saucepan with the water and bring to the boil.
2. Sift the flour and salt together and add all at once to the pan. Stir quickly with a wooden spoon until the mixture is smooth and leaves the sides of the pan clean. Remove from the heat, spread the paste over the base of the pan and leave to cool slightly.
3. Gradually beat in the eggs a little at a time until the mixture is smooth and glossy.
4. Either put heaped teaspoons of the mixture on to the baking sheets or put the mixture into a piping bag fitted with a 1–2 cm (½–¾ inch) plain nozzle and pipe out buns about the size of a walnut or a little larger if preferred.
5. Cook in a hot oven for about 25 minutes (30–40 minutes for larger buns) or until well risen, firm and golden brown. Remove from the oven and make a slit in each bun to allow the steam to escape, then return to the oven for 3–4 minutes to dry out.
6. Cool on a wire rack and when cold pack in a rigid container and freeze (or open freeze and then pack). Store for up to 3 months.
7. Thaw out slowly (2–3 hours). The buns may need to be refreshed in a moderate oven (180°C, 350°F, Gas Mark 4) for about 5 minutes before use.

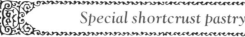

Special shortcrust pastry

225 g (8 oz) self-raising flour
pinch of salt
25 g (1 oz) caster sugar (optional)
50 g (2 oz) butter
50 g (2 oz) block margarine
25 g (1 oz) lard
1 egg yolk
milk, to mix

Preparation time: *about 10 minutes*

This crisp and crumbly mouthwatering pastry made with self-raising flour breaks all the rules, but gives a special taste and texture to all sweet pies, large or small.

1. Sift the flour, salt and sugar, if using, into a mixing bowl. Rub in the butter, margarine and lard with the fingertips until the mixture resembles fine breadcrumbs.
2. Add the egg yolk and enough milk to mix a pliable dough, using a round-bladed knife.
3. Turn the dough on to a lightly floured board or work surface and knead lightly until smooth and even.
4. Wrap in a freezer polythene bag or foil and freeze for up to 1 month. Thaw for 2–3 hours at room temperature.

LEFT: Smoked salmon and asparagus quiche RIGHT: Pissaladière

Smoked salmon and asparagus quiche

Serves 6

225 g (8 oz) shortcrust or wholemeal pastry made with 225 g (8 oz) plain flour (page 16)	3 eggs
	300 ml (½ pint) single cream
	4 tablespoons milk
1 × 425 g (15 oz) can green asparagus spears, drained	salt
	freshly ground black pepper
175 g (6 oz) smoked salmon pieces or trimmings, roughly chopped	50 g (2 oz) Lancashire cheese, grated
	25 g (1 oz) fresh white breadcrumbs

Preparation time: *20 minutes*
Cooking time: *about 45 minutes*
Oven: *220°C, 425°F, Gas Mark 7*
then: *190°C, 375°F, Gas Mark 5*

1. Roll out the pastry on a lightly floured board or work surface and use to line a 23–25 cm (9–10 inch) flan ring, dish or tin. Lay the smoked salmon in the base. Reserve the tips of 6 asparagus spears for the garnish; chop the remainder and lay over the salmon.

2. Whisk the eggs with the cream, milk, salt and plenty of pepper and pour into the flan case. Combine the cheese and breadcrumbs and sprinkle evenly over the surface.

3. Stand the quiche on a baking sheet and bake in a preheated hot oven for 20 minutes. Reduce the oven temperature and bake for a further 25 minutes or until the filling is well risen and golden brown. **F**

4. Allow to cool completely. Wrap in foil or cling film and store carefully in the freezer. Thaw for 8–12 hours. Serve hot or cold. Use the reserved asparagus tips to garnish the quiche. If liked, garnish also with tiny rolls of smoked salmon.

Dundee cake

225 g (8 oz) plain flour	225 g (8 oz) butter
1 teaspoon mixed spice	225 g (8 oz) soft brown
50 g (2 oz) blanched	sugar, light or dark
almonds, chopped	4 eggs
225 g (8 oz) currants	1–2 tablespoons lemon
225 g (8 oz) sultanas	juice
225 g (8 oz) raisins, seedless	50 g (2 oz) whole blanched
or stoned	almonds
100 g (4 oz) cut mixed peel	
grated rind of 1 orange and	
1 lemon	

Preparation time: *40 minutes, plus cooling*
Cooking time: *2½–3 hours*
Oven: *160°C, 325°F, Gas Mark 3*

This is lighter than the traditional Christmas cake, but with its famous topping of whole blanched almonds it is good for those who dislike marzipan and icing. It may be pierced and sprinkled with 3–4 tablespoons brandy before wrapping in foil, like Christmas cake. Dundee cake can be made 2–3 weeks before required or up to 4 months in advance if stored in the freezer.

1. Grease a 20 cm (8 inch) round deep cake tin and line with greased greaseproof paper. Sift the flour and spice together.
2. Mix together the almonds, currants, sultanas, raisins, mixed peel and orange and lemon rind.
3. Cream the butter and sugar together in a mixing bowl until very light, pale and fluffy. Beat in the eggs one at a time, folding in a tablespoon of flour after each addition.
4. Fold in the remaining flour followed by the dried fruit mixture and enough lemon juice to give a dropping consistency.
5. Turn the mixture into the prepared tin and make a slight hollow in the centre. Arrange the whole blanched almonds in circles over the top of the cake. Bake in a preheated moderate oven for 2½–3 hours or until a warmed fine skewer inserted into the centre of the cake comes out clean. Cover the cake with a sheet of foil if it appears to be overbrowning during baking.
6. Cool in the tin for about 15 minutes then turn on to a wire rack and leave to cool completely. Store wrapped in foil.

Petits fours

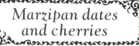
Marzipan dates and cherries

Fill the stone cavities of dates, glacé cherries or no-need-to-soak prunes with small pieces of marzipan. Criss-cross the top of the marzipan decoratively, using a small sharp knife. The fruits may then be rolled in granulated sugar, if liked for a crunchy sweet covering.

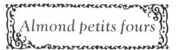
Almond petits fours

	75 g (3 oz) caster sugar
	a few drops of almond
	essence
Makes 20–24	glacé cherries or angelica,
2 egg whites	chopped, to decorate
175 g (6 oz) ground	
almonds	

Preparation time: *20 minutes*
Cooking time: *about 20 minutes*
Oven: *150°C, 300°F, Gas Mark 2*

1. Line 2 baking sheets with non-stick silicone paper or rice paper.
2. Whisk the egg whites until stiff peaks form and fold in the ground almonds, sugar and almond essence using a large metal spoon.
3. Place the mixture in a piping bag fitted with a 1 cm (½ inch) star nozzle and pipe small stars, whirls or fingers on to the prepared baking sheets. Decorate each with a small piece of glacé cherry or angelica.
4. Bake in a preheated low oven for 15–20 minutes or until just beginning to colour. Transfer to a wire rack and leave to cool completely. Store in an airtight container.

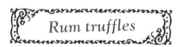
Rum truffles

	300 g (10 oz) icing sugar,
	sifted
Makes approx 450 g (1 lb)	100 g (4 oz) unsalted butter,
100 g (4 oz) plain chocolate	softened
	1–2 teaspoons rum
	chocolate vermicelli

Preparation time: *about 20 minutes*

1. Melt the chocolate in a heatproof bowl over a saucepan of barely simmering water. Gradually add the sugar and softened butter and whisk until smooth. Flavour with the rum.
2. Form the mixture into small balls, roll in chocolate vermicelli and leave to set for 4–5 hours. Store in an airtight container. Serve in paper sweet cases. Some of the balls can be left smooth, if liked.

Mayonnaise

Makes about 400 ml (14 fl oz)

2 egg yolks

½ teaspoon made English mustard

300 ml (½ pint) olive oil

about 2 tablespoons lemon juice

2–3 tablespoons white wine vinegar

salt

white pepper

about 1 teaspoon caster sugar

Preparation time: *about 25 minutes*

The eggs must be at room temperature: if they are taken straight from the refrigerator the mayonnaise will curdle.

1. Put the egg yolks and mustard into a warmed bowl and mix thoroughly.

2. Whisk in half the oil drop by drop, using a hand or electric hand mixer, until thick. Whisk in 1 tablespoon lemon juice. Then whisk in the rest of the oil in the same way, a slow trickle.

3. Add vinegar, lemon juice, sugar and salt and pepper to taste and store in an airtight container in the refrigerator for up to 3 weeks.

CLOCKWISE FROM FRONT: *Almond petits fours, Rum truffles and Marzipan dates, Dundee cake*

Christmas Eve

Beef and Pheasant Casserole

Mincemeat and Apple
Lattice Pie

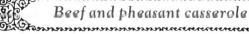

Beef and pheasant casserole

1 oven-ready pheasant jointed into 8 pieces	450 ml (¾ pint) beef stock
450 g (1 lb) best-quality braising steak, trimmed of excess fat and cut into 2.5 cm (1 inch) cubes	1 tablespoon red wine vinegar
	salt
	freshly ground black pepper
2 tablespoons vegetable oil or dripping	½ teaspoon dried thyme
2 large onions, peeled and cut into eighths	4 tablespoons cranberry sauce
2 tablespoons plain flour	100 g (4 oz) button mushrooms, sliced
150 ml (¼ pint) dry white wine	

Preparation time: *30 minutes*
Cooking time: *2¼ hours*
Oven: *160°C, 325°F, Gas Mark 3*

1. Heat the oil in a frying pan, add the pheasant pieces and fry over a moderate heat, turning often, until well browned. Transfer to a casserole.
2. Reheat the oil in the pan, add the beef cubes and fry, turning often, until well sealed and browned on all sides. Add to the casserole.
3. Add the onions to the pan and fry over a gentle heat for 5 minutes until lightly coloured. Sprinkle in the flour, stir well and fry for a further 1–2 minutes. Gradually stir in the wine, stock and vinegar and bring to the boil. Season well with salt and pepper, add the thyme and cranberry sauce and heat gently, stirring, until the sauce has melted.
4. Pour the contents of the pan into the casserole, cover and cook in a preheated moderate oven for about 2 hours or until the pheasant and beef are tender. Add the mushrooms 30 minutes before the end of the cooking time. Taste and adjust the seasoning. [F] Serve with creamed potatoes and Brussels sprouts.

[F] Cool the casserole quickly, transfer to a rigid container and freeze for up to 6 weeks. Thaw overnight at cool room temperature. Reheat in a covered casserole at 180°C, 350°F, Gas Mark 4 for 50–60 minutes.

Mincemeat and apple lattice pie

Serves 5–6	2 tablespoons brandy (optional)
225 g (8 oz) Special shortcrust pastry (page 18)	
	2 tablespoons apricot jam
450 g (1 lb) cooking apples, peeled, cored and sliced	2 teaspoons water
225 g (8 oz) mincemeat	a little egg white or milk, to glaze

Preparation time: *20 minutes*
Cooking time: *about 40 minutes*
Oven: *200°C, 400°F, Gas Mark 6*

1. Roll out the pastry on a lightly floured board or work surface and use to line a 22–23 cm (8½–9 inch) round shallow pie dish. Reserve the pastry trimmings.
2. Arrange half the apple slices in the pastry case. Cover evenly with the mincemeat, sprinkle with the brandy, if using, and cover with the remaining apple slices.
3. Melt the apricot jam with the water in a small saucepan and brush over the apples. Roll out the reserved pastry trimmings and cut into narrow strips. Twist these and lay over the apple, dampening the ends to seal them to the edge of the pie.
4. Brush the pastry lattice and the edge of the pie with egg white or milk, stand on a preheated baking sheet and bake in a preheated hot oven for about 35 minutes or until the pastry is well browned. [F]
5. Serve hot or cold with whipped cream and brandy butter.

[F] Freeze for up to 2 months.

LEFT: Mincemeat and apple lattice pie RIGHT: Beef and pheasant casserole

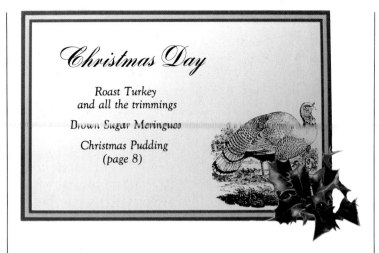

Christmas Day

Roast Turkey
and all the trimmings

Brown Sugar Meringues

Christmas Pudding
(page 8)

Roast turkey

Serves 8

4.5–5.5 kg (10–12 lb) oven-ready turkey, with giblets	**ACCOMPANIMENTS:**
1 onion, peeled and quartered	**450 g (1 lb) chipolata sausages**
pâté and chestnut stuffing (page 16)	**8–16 streaky bacon rashers, rinded, boned and rolled**
40 g (1½ oz) butter or margarine, softened	**gravy**
2 tablespoons vegetable oil	**TO GARNISH:**
salt	**watercress or parsley sprigs**
freshly ground black pepper	

Preparation time: *about 30 minutes*
Cooking time: *3–3¼ hours*
Oven: *180°C, 350°F, Gas Mark 4*

1. Put the turkey giblets into a saucepan with half the onion and pour in cold water to cover. Bring to the boil, then lower heat, cover and simmer for 1 hour. Strain the stock and reserve.

2. Stuff the neck end only of the turkey with the stuffing mixture. Secure the neck flap with a skewer and lightly truss the bird. Place the remaining onion in the body cavity.

3. Place the turkey in a roasting tin and rub all over with butter. Add the oil to the tin and season the turkey with salt and pepper.

4. Roast in a preheated moderate oven for 3–3¼ hours, basting from time to time. Cover with greaseproof paper or foil when sufficiently browned. Check for doneness by inserting a skewer into the thickest part of the thigh, when the juices should run clear: if pink, cook the turkey for a further 15 minutes and test again.

5. Grill the chipolatas and bacon rolls about 15 minutes before required and keep warm. Make bread sauce if using.

6. Transfer the turkey to a large carving dish. Drain off the fat from the tin and use the juices and reserved giblet stock to make gravy.

7. Arrange the turkey on a large serving dish and surround with roast potatoes, chipolatas and bacon rolls. Garnish with watercress or parsley sprigs. Serve with Brussels sprouts, gravy and cranberry sauce handed separately.

A Prepare the giblet stock up to 24 hours in advance, strain and chill.

LEFT TO RIGHT: Christmas pudding (page 8), Brown sugar meringues, Roast turkey served with Brussels sprouts and cranberry sauce

Brown sugar meringues

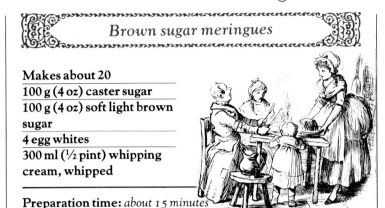

Makes about 20

100 g (4 oz) caster sugar

100 g (4 oz) soft light brown sugar

4 egg whites

300 ml (½ pint) whipping cream, whipped

Preparation time: *about 15 minutes*
Cooking time: *about 2 hours*
Oven: 120°C, 250°F, Gas Mark ½

1. Line 2 baking sheets with non-stick silicone paper. Sift the sugars together twice. Put the egg whites in a grease-free bowl and whisk until stiff, dry and standing in peaks.
2. Whisk in the sugars a little at a time, making sure the meringue is stiff again before the next addition.
3. Put the meringue mixture into a piping bag fitted with a star vegetable nozzle. Pipe into fingers or whirls on the baking sheet.
4. Bake in a preheated very cool oven for about 2 hours, reversing the baking sheets after an hour, until the meringues are firm and dry and may easily be moved from the paper. Remove from the oven and leave to cool completely, then store in an airtight container.
5. Sandwich the meringues together with cream. Serve with a bowl of frozen or canned raspberries, thawed.

Boxing Day

Winter Salad

Potatoes in cream sauce

Old Fashioned Game Pie

Caramelized Oranges

Winter salad

Serves 8	50–75 g (2–3 oz) shelled
2 green-skinned dessert	walnuts
apples	4 spring onions, trimmed
2 red-skinned dessert	and finely sliced
apples	4 tablespoons French
2 conference pears	dressing
2 tablespoons lemon juice	2 tablespoons single cream
1 head celery, trimmed and	
sliced	

Preparation time: *about 20 minutes*

1. Core and slice the apples and place in a large bowl. Peel, core and slice the pears and add to the bowl with the lemon juice. Stir lightly but thoroughly to mix, then drain off the excess lemon juice.
2. Add the celery, walnuts and onions. Mix the French dressing and cream together and, whisking with a fork, pour over the salad. Toss lightly but thoroughly with 2 salad spoons then turn into a salad bowl, cover with cling film and chill in the refrigerator until required.

Potatoes in cream sauce

Serves 8	150 ml (¼ pint) cream
1.25 kg (2½ lb) potatoes,	freshly ground black
peeled	pepper
salt	freshly ground nutmeg
40 g (1½ oz) butter	2 tablespoons chopped
40 g (1½ oz) plain flour	fresh parsley
300 ml (½ pint) milk	

Old-fashioned game pie

Serves 6–8	salt
40 g (1½ oz) butter	freshly ground black
2 oven-ready pheasants,	pepper
quartered	1 bay leaf
2 pigeons or partridges,	1 tablespoon cornflour
halved	2 tablespoons port or sherry
350 g (12 oz) bacon rashers,	3 tablespoons redcurrant
rinded and diced	jelly
2 large onions, sliced	225 g (8 oz) puff pastry
3 large carrots, sliced	made with 225 g (8 oz) plain
4 celery sticks, sliced	flour (page 16)
600 ml (1 pint) beef stock	beaten egg, to glaze
225 ml (8 fl oz) red wine	

Preparation time: *about 45 minutes, plus cooling time*
Cooking time: *about 2 hours*
Oven: *220°C, 425°F, Gas Mark 7*
then: *190°C, 375°F, Gas Mark 5*

1. Melt the butter in a large pan, add the pheasant and partridge and fry over moderate heat until browned, then remove. Add the bacon and onions and brown lightly.
2. Return the pheasant and partridge pieces to the pan with the carrots, celery, stock and wine. Bring to the boil, season well and add the bay leaf. Cover and simmer for 1–1½ hours until tender.
3. Strain off the juices into a small pan. Cool the meat slightly, then remove the flesh from the bones and place in a pie dish with the bacon and vegetables.
4. Blend the cornflour with the port and stir into the juices with the redcurrant jelly. Bring to the boil, stirring until slightly reduced. Pour into the pie dish.
5. Roll out the pastry slightly larger than the top of the pie dish. Cut off a strip 2.5 cm (1 inch) wide and fit on to the dampened rim of the pie dish. Brush the pastry rim with beaten egg and cover with the pastry lid. Press the edges firmly together, then trim and flute.
6. Roll out the pastry trimmings and use to cut into leaves. Brush the pastry lid with beaten egg, make a hole in the centre and decorate with pastry leaves.
7. Stand the pie on a baking sheet and bake in a pre-heated oven for about 20 minutes. Reduce temperature and bake for 20–30 minutes until well browned.

Preparation time: *15 minutes*
Cooking time: *about 25 minutes*

1. Boil the potatoes in salted water until just tender, drain and cube. Place in a serving dish.
2. Melt the butter in a pan, add flour and stir for 1 minute. Remove from heat and stir in milk and cream. Bring to the boil, then simmer over low heat for 2 minutes. Add salt, pepper and nutmeg. Pour over potatoes and sprinkle with parsley.

Caramelized oranges

Serves 8

16 medium oranges

450 g (1 lb) granulated sugar

300 ml (½ pint) water

8 whole cloves

Preparation time: *about 1 hour, plus chilling*

1. Thinly pare the rind from 5 of the oranges and remove all the pith. Cut the rind into narrow strips and place in a small saucepan. Cover with cold water and bring to the boil, then lower the heat and simmer for 10 minutes or until tender. Drain, reserving 4 tablespoons of the cooking liquid.

2. Cut the peel and pith away from the remaining oranges, reserving any juice. Stand all the oranges in a bowl in a single layer.

3. Put the sugar, water and cloves into a heavy-based saucepan and heat gently until the sugar dissolves, stirring frequently, then boil hard without further stirring until the syrup turns a caramel colour. Remove from the heat immediately and stir in the reserved orange liquid and any reserved orange juice.

4. Heat the syrup gently, then pour over the oranges. Cover and chill in the refrigerator for at least 12 hours and preferably 1–2 days, turning the fruit in the syrup occasionally.

5. Before serving cut each orange crossways into slices and reassemble, spearing each with a wooden cocktail stick through the centre if necessary. Place in a serving dish and pour over the syrup, then sprinkle with the strips of orange rind. Serve with cream.

CLOCKWISE FROM FRONT: *Caramelized oranges, Old-fashioned game pie, Mince pies (page 11), Potatoes in cream sauce, Winter salad*

Supper for 10

Carrot and Coriander Soup

Herb Bread

Curried Turkey Drogheda

Tomato, Bean and Artichoke Salad

Rum Syllabubs with Brandy
Snaps

Gingered Gâteau

Carrot and coriander soup

Serves 10	freshly ground black
75 g (3 oz) butter or	pepper
margarine	1 tablespoon ground
225 g (8 oz) onions, peeled	coriander seeds
and chopped	1 bay leaf
750 g (1½ lb) carrots,	1 tablespoon lemon juice
scraped and sliced	600 ml (1 pint) milk
3 tablespoons plain flour	150 ml (¼ pint) single
1.2 litres (2 pints) chicken	cream
stock	2 tablespoons chopped
salt	fresh parsley, to garnish

Preparation time: *20 minutes*
Cooking time: *about 40 minutes*

1. Melt the butter in a large saucepan. Add the onions and fry over a gentle heat for about 5 minutes or until soft and lightly coloured. Add the carrots, stir to coat in butter, and fry for a further 2–3 minutes.
2. Stir in the flour and cook for 1–2 minutes, then gradually stir in the stock and bring to the boil.
3. Season well with salt and pepper and add the coriander, bay leaf and lemon juice. Cover the pan and simmer gently for about 30 minutes or until the carrots are very tender.
4. Discard the bay leaf and purée the soup in a food processor or blender, or pass through a sieve. [F]
5. Return to a clean pan with the milk and return to the boil. Taste and adjust the seasoning, stir in the cream and reheat gently. Serve at once in warmed soup bowls, garnished with chopped parsley. Serve with herb bread (see below).

[F] Freeze for up to 3 months. Thaw the soup in a saucepan over gentle heat and continue from step 5.

Herb bread

	2 tablespoons dried mixed
	herbs
1 long French loaf	salt
175 g (6 oz) butter	freshly ground black
1 clove garlic, peeled and	pepper
crushed	

Preparation time: *10 minutes*
Cooking time: *about 15 minutes*
Oven: *200°C, 400°F, Gas Mark 6*

1. Cut the loaf diagonally into slices about 2.5 cm (1 inch) thick, without cutting through the bottom crust.
2. Beat the butter in a bowl until soft and creamy, then beat in the garlic, herbs, salt and pepper. Spread the herb butter on both sides of each slice of bread.
3. Wrap the loaf in foil and bake in a preheated hot oven for 10–15 minutes. Serve hot, cut into slices.

Curried turkey drogheda

Serves 10	900 g–1.25 kg (2–2½ lb)
450 g (1 lb) long-grain rice	cooked turkey meat, diced
salt	225 g (8 oz) garlic sausage,
3 tablespoons chopped	sliced
fresh parsley	1 × 425 g (15 oz) can
grated rind of 1 lemon	pineapple pieces, drained
200 ml (7 fl oz) mayonnaise	1 × 425 g (15 oz) can sliced
(page 21)	mangoes, drained and
6 tablespoons French	roughly chopped
dressing	1 bunch spring onions,
1½–2 teaspoons curry	trimmed and chopped
powder	225 g (8 oz) cooked peas
freshly ground black	8–10 celery sticks, sliced
pepper	mustard and cress

Preparation time: *about 40 minutes, plus chilling*

1. Cook the rice in a large saucepan of boiling salted water for 15–20 minutes or until just tender. Drain and rinse under cold running water, then drain again. Turn into a bowl and mix in the parsley and lemon rind.
2. In a large bowl combine the mayonnaise and French dressing with curry powder and salt and pepper to taste.
3. Add the turkey meat and turn in the dressing to coat thoroughly. Chop half the garlic sausage and add to the bowl with all the remaining ingredients. Mix lightly to coat evenly. Cover and chill for at least 1 hour.
4. Arrange the rice around the edge of a large serving dish and spoon the turkey mixture into the centre.
5. Roll the remaining slices of garlic sausage into cornets and arrange around the edge of the salad on the rice. Garnish with mustard and cress.

Tomato, bean and artichoke salad

Serves 10

750 g (1½ lb) stringless French beans, topped and tailed

~alt

2 × 425 g (15 oz) cans artichoke hearts, drained

150 ml (¼ pint) French dressing

freshly ground black pepper

750 g (1½ lb) tomatoes, quartered

Preparation time: *20 minutes*
Cooking time: *5 minutes*

1. Cook the beans in a large saucepan of boiling salted water for 3–5 minutes. Drain and cool. Cut the beans into 5 cm (2 inch) lengths and place in a bowl.

2. Cut the artichoke hearts into quarters and add to the beans with the dressing and salt and pepper. Toss lightly but thoroughly and transfer to a large dish. Arrange the tomato wedges around the edge of the dish.

3. Cover with cling film until ready to serve.

CLOCKWISE FROM LEFT: *Curried turkey drogheda, Herb bread, Carrot and coriander soup, Tomato, bean and artichoke salad*

Rum syllabubs

Serves 6–8

150 ml (¼ pint) medium white wine

finely grated rind of 1 orange

4 tablespoons caster sugar

4–5 tablespoons rum or Cointreau

600 ml (1 pint) double cream

Preparation time: *10 minutes, plus soaking and chilling*

1. Put the wine, orange rind and sugar in a large bowl, stir to mix and leave to stand for about 1 hour.
2. Add the rum or Cointreau and then gradually pour in the cream. Whisk until the mixture stands in soft peaks.
3. Pour into 6–8 glasses and chill in the refrigerator for up to 30 minutes. Serve with brandy snaps.

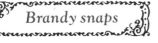

Brandy snaps

Makes 12–16

50 g (2 oz) butter

50 g (2 oz) golden syrup

50 g (2 oz) caster sugar

50 g (2 oz) plain flour

¼ teaspoon ground ginger

Preparation time: *30 minutes*
Cooking time: *about 30 minutes*
Oven: *160°C, 325°F, Gas Mark 3*

1. Line several baking sheets with non-stick silicone paper and grease several wooden spoon handles or cream horn tins.
2. Melt the butter in a saucepan with the golden syrup and sugar, then remove from the heat.
3. Sift the flour and ginger together and beat into the melted mixture.
4. Place teaspoons of the mixture well apart on the baking sheets and spread out a little. Bake in a moderate oven for 8–10 minutes or until golden brown.
5. Cool until just firm enough to remove with a palette knife, then immediately wind round the spoon handles or cream horn tins. If the ginger snaps become too brittle before winding, return to the oven for a minute or so and try again. Leave to cool on a wire rack until firm, then slide off the handles or cream horn tins.

Gingered gâteau

Serves 8

4 eggs

100 g (4 oz) caster sugar

100 g (4 oz) plain flour

¼ teaspoon ground ginger

¼ teaspoon mixed spice

25 g (1 oz) butter, melted and cooled

icing sugar, sifted

FILLING:

450 ml (¾ pint) double or whipping cream

4–6 tablespoons ginger marmalade

1 × 300 g (11 oz) can mandarin orange segments, drained

a few pieces of stem ginger, (optional)

Preparation time: *about 30 minutes, plus cooling*
Cooking time: *about 20 minutes*
Oven: *190°C, 375°F, Gas Mark 5*

1. Grease a 30 × 25 cm (12 × 10 inch) Swiss roll tin and line with greased greaseproof paper. Lightly dredge with flour.
2. Put the eggs and sugar into a large heatproof bowl. Place the bowl over a saucepan of gently simmering water and whisk until the mixture is thick and the whisk leaves a thick trail when lifted. Remove from the heat. (If using an electric mixer, no heat is needed.)
3. Sift the flour, ginger and spice together twice and fold lightly and evenly into the egg mixture. Finally fold in the cooled butter using a large metal spoon.
4. Pour the mixture into the prepared tin and spread out lightly, making sure the corners are well filled. Bake in a preheated moderately hot oven for 15–20 minutes or until pale brown and just firm and springy to the touch.
5. Turn the sponge on to a sheet of greaseproof or non-stick silicone paper lightly sprinkled with icing sugar. Peel off the lining paper immediately and trim the edges of the sponge neatly with a sharp knife. While still warm roll up from a short edge, with the paper inside. Leave to cool completely on a wire rack.
6. Whip the cream until stiff. Reserve 2 tablespoons and fold the ginger marmalade into the remainder.
7. Unroll the sponge carefully and remove the paper. Spread the ginger cream over the sponge. Reserve 8 of the best mandarin orange segments for decoration and arrange the remainder over the ginger cream. Re-roll the sponge carefully, dredge with icing sugar and place on a serving dish.
8. Put the reserved cream in a piping bag fitted with a star nozzle. Pipe a line of cream down the centre of the roll. Decorate with the remaining mandarins and pieces of stem ginger, if using. Chill in the refrigerator until ready to serve.

FRONT: Gingered gâteau BACK: Rum syllabubs with brandy snaps

New Year's Eve

Beansprout Salad

Smoked Mackerel and Olive Pâté

Chinese Lettuce Salad

Lasagne Verde

Chestnut Profiteroles

Lemon and Lime Soufflé

An attractive assortment of supper dishes for the traditional New Year's Eve party. The profiteroles and the soufflé can be made in advance and frozen until required.

Beansprout salad

100 g (4 oz) button mushrooms, thinly sliced	4 carrots, scraped and cut into thin sticks
2 tablespoons French dressing	225 g (8 oz) red cabbage, thinly shredded
2 cartons fresh bean-sprouts or 2 × 425 g (15 oz) cans bean-sprouts, well drained	3 cartons mustard and cress

Preparation time: *20 minutes, plus standing*

1. Put the mushrooms in a large salad bowl and pour over the French dressing. Leave to stand for 30 minutes.
2. Add all the remaining ingredients and toss well. Serve immediately.

Smoked mackerel and olive pâté

Serves 20

1 onion, peeled and chopped	freshly ground black pepper
4 hard-boiled eggs, shelled and chopped	1–2 garlic cloves, peeled and crushed
12 stuffed green olives, sliced	12 tablespoons plain unsweetened yogurt
750 g (1½ lb) smoked mackerel fillets, skinned and chopped	TO GARNISH:
	2 tablespoons chopped fresh parsley
salt	16 stuffed green olives, sliced

Preparation time: *about 30 minutes*

1. Put the onion and hard-boiled eggs into a food processor or blender and process until thoroughly chopped. Add the olives and smoked mackerel and process again until smooth.
2. Season well with salt and pepper, add the garlic and yogurt and process again until smooth.
3. Turn the mixture into a bowl, taste and adjust the seasoning, and stir well. (If too thick add more yogurt.)
4. Turn the pâté into 2 serving dishes and sprinkle with chopped parsley. Arrange sliced olives around the edge.

Chinese lettuce salad

2 green-skinned dessert apples, peeled, cored and thinly sliced	1 bunch spring onions, trimmed and chopped
2 tablespoons lemon juice	1 head celery, trimmed and thinly sliced
2 heads Chinese leaves, trimmed and finely sliced	2 bunches watercress, trimmed
1 unpeeled cucumber, diced	300 ml (½ pint) French dressing
2 green peppers, seeded, cored and thinly sliced	

Preparation time: *about 30–40 minutes*

1. Put the apple slices in a large salad bowl with the lemon juice, toss to coat thoroughly, then drain.
2. Add all the remaining salad ingredients and toss well. Cover with cling film and chill in the refrigerator until ready to serve. Pour over the French dressing and toss again just before serving.

FROM THE FRONT: Smoked mackerel and olive pâté, Chinese lettuce salad, Beansprout salad, Lasagne verde

Lasagne

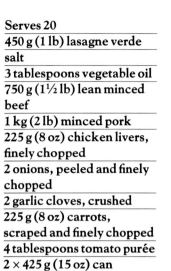

Serves 20

450 g (1 lb) lasagne verde	2 tablespoons Worcestershire sauce
salt	½ teaspoon ground nutmeg
3 tablespoons vegetable oil	225 g (8 oz) button mushrooms, chopped (optional)
750 g (1½ lb) lean minced beef	
1 kg (2 lb) minced pork	freshly ground black pepper
225 g (8 oz) chicken livers, finely chopped	SAUCE:
2 onions, peeled and finely chopped	100 g (4 oz) butter or margarine
2 garlic cloves, crushed	100 g (4 oz) plain flour
225 g (8 oz) carrots, scraped and finely chopped	1.2 litres (2 pints) milk
4 tablespoons tomato purée	2 teaspoons English mustard powder
2 × 425 g (15 oz) can tomatoes	225 g (8 oz) mature Cheddar cheese, grated
450 ml (¾ pint) tomato juice	

Preparation time: *about 45 minutes*
Cooking time: *about 1½ hours*
Oven: *200°C, 400°F, Gas Mark 6*

1. Cook the lasagne 3–4 sheets at a time in a large saucepan of boiling salted water to which 1 tablespoon of the oil has been added, for about 6 minutes or until just tender. Drain well and lay out on trays.
2. Put the minced beef and pork in a large, heavy-based saucepan with the remaining oil and cook until the fat runs, stirring frequently. Add the chicken livers, onions, garlic and carrots and cook gently for about 10 minutes, stirring frequently.
3. Stir in the tomato purée, the tomatoes with their juice and the Worcestershire sauce, nutmeg and mushrooms. Season well with salt and pepper. Bring to the boil, cover and simmer gently for 30 minutes. Stir occasionally and taste, adjusting the seasoning if necessary.
4. Make the sauce: melt the butter in a saucepan, stir in the flour and cook for 1–2 minutes. Remove from the heat and gradually stir in the milk, then bring to the boil, stirring frequently, and simmer for 2 minutes. Season well with salt and pepper, then stir in the mustard and 150 g (5 oz) of the cheese and stir until the cheese is melted.
5. Lightly oil 2 large baking dishes about 5 cm (2 inches) deep. Beginning with a layer of lasagne, make layers of lasagne, meat sauce and cheese sauce, ending with cheese sauce. Sprinkle with the remaining grated cheese. F
6. Bake towards the top of a preheated hot oven for about 40–50 minutes or until well browned on top. Reverse the dishes halfway through the cooking time. Serve hot.

Chestnut profiteroles

Serves 12–14

choux pastry made with
125 g (5 oz) plain flour
(page 10)

FILLING:
1 × 225 g (8 oz) can
sweetened chestnut purée
or chestnut spread

2 tablespoons rum
450 ml (¾ pint) whipping
cream

CARAMEL:
225 g (8 oz) granulated
sugar
150 ml (¼ pint) water

Preparation time: *about 1 hour*
Cooking time: *about 45 minutes*
Oven: *220°C, 425°F, Gas Mark 7*

1. Make and bake the choux pastry buns as described on page 18. Cool completely on a wire rack.
2. Make the filling: beat the chestnut purée and rum together until smooth.
3. Whip the cream until stiff and fold into the chestnut mixture. Put the chestnut cream into a piping bag fitted with a plain 5 mm (¼ inch) nozzle.
4. Pipe the filling into the buns and leave on a wire rack.
5. Make the caramel: put the sugar and water in a heavy-based saucepan and stir until the sugar is dissolved, then boil without further stirring until a light caramel colour. Remove from the heat and dip the top of each bun into the caramel or drizzle a little over each one, using a teaspoon. Leave to set. Do not add the caramel more than 2 hours before serving.
6. Serve the chestnut profiteroles in a shallow dish, piled one on top of the other.

Lemon and lime soufflé

Serves 12–14

6 eggs, separated
400 g (14 oz) caster sugar
grated rind and juice of 3
lemons
grated rind and juice of 1
lime

2 × 15 g (½ oz) sachets
powdered gelatine
5 tablespoons water
450 ml (¾ pint) double or
whipping cream
lime or kiwi fruit slices, to
decorate

Preparation time: *about 40 minutes, plus setting overnight*

The soufflé may also be set in a 3-pint soufflé dish which has a collar made of non-stick silicone paper tied around the dish so it comes 5 cm (2 inches) above the rim of the dish. Fill the dish to about 2.5 cm (1 inch) above the rim.

1. Put the egg yolks in a large bowl with the sugar and the lemon and lime rinds and juices. Whisk until very thick and creamy and the whisk leaves a heavy trail in the mixture when lifted. Alternatively, set the bowl over a saucepan of gently simmering water and whisk by hand until thick.
2. Sprinkle the gelatine over the water in a bowl and leave until spongy, then set over a pan of hot water until completely melted. Allow to cool a little, then whisk the gelatine liquid into the egg mixture. Leave until on the point of setting.
3. Whisk the egg whites until very stiff. Whisk half the cream until soft peaks form.
4. Using a large metal spoon, fold first the cream, then the egg whites into the lemon and lime mixture, until thoroughly blended. Turn into one or two glass serving bowls and chill overnight until set. [F] If freezing, do not use glass bowls.
5. Whip the remaining cream until stiff and use to decorate the top of the soufflé(s), together with lime slices.

[F] This soufflé will freeze well for up to 2 months. Allow to thaw overnight in a cool place and then add the decoration.

LEFT: Chestnut profiteroles RIGHT: Lemon and lime soufflé

New Year's Day Drinks Party

White Wine Cup ~ Christmas Mull
Stilton Dip with Cheese Sablées
Prune, Almond and Bacon Rolls
Celery and Peanut Boats
Smoked Cod's Roe Pinwheels
Cheese and Anchovy Twists
Cocktail canapes
Curry Puffs with Watercress

Christmas mull

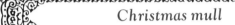

Makes about 16 glasses	1 teaspoon cardamom
2 bottles burgundy or heavy red wine	seeds (optional)
¼ bottle gin	5 cm (2 inch) piece cinnamon stick
75 g (3 oz) seedless raisins	thinly pared rind of 2 lemons
100 g (4 oz) caster sugar	
8 whole cloves	

Preparation time: *15 minutes*
Cooking time: *about 40 minutes*

1. Put the wine, half the gin and all the remaining ingredients into a large saucepan.
2. Heat gently, stirring, until the sugar has dissolved, then bring to the boil. Turn the heat to the lowest setting and simmer very gently for at least 30 minutes. Stir in remaining gin, reheat and serve at once.

Stilton dip with cheese sablées

175 g (6 oz) Stilton, rind removed	1 teaspoon paprika
1 small onion, peeled and chopped	1 teaspoon sugar
2 celery sticks, chopped	1 tablespoon lemon juice
1 hard-boiled egg, chopped	1 tablespoon white wine vinegar
salt	4–6 tablespoons vegetable oil

Preparation time: *about 10 minutes, plus cooling*

1. Put the Stilton, onion, celery and hard-boiled egg in a food processor or blender and process until smooth. Add all the remaining ingredients and process again until smooth. Taste and adjust the seasoning and turn into a small serving bowl.
2. Serve with cheese sablées (see below) and a plate of crudités such as sticks of celery and carrot, strips of green pepper and small florets of raw cauliflower.

Cheese sablées

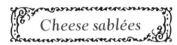

150 g (6 oz) plain flour	65 g (2½ oz) mature Cheddar cheese, grated
a pinch of salt	15 g (½ oz) Parmesan cheese, grated
freshly ground black pepper	1 egg yolk
cayenne	1 tablespoon water
100 g (4 oz) butter, diced	milk, to glaze
	2 tablespoons finely chopped walnuts

Preparation time: *about 15 minutes, plus chilling and cooling*
Cooking time: *about 15 minutes*
Oven: *190°C, 375°F, Gas Mark 5*

1. Sift the flour with the salt, pepper and cayenne to taste into a mixing bowl. Add the butter and rub in with the fingertips until the mixture resembles fine breadcrumbs. Mix in the cheeses and stir in the egg yolk and water to bind.
2. Shape into a roll about 2.5 cm (1 inch) in diameter and wrap in foil or cling film. Chill in the refrigerator until firm. **F**
3. Cut into 5 mm (¼ inch) slices and place on baking sheets lined with non-stick silicone paper. Brush with milk and sprinkle with walnuts.
4. Bake in a preheated moderately hot oven for 10–12 minutes. Transfer to a wire tray and leave to cool completely, then store in an airtight container.
F Can be frozen at this stage. Allow to thaw until just able to be cut with a sharp knife and proceed as step 3.

CLOCKWISE FROM THE BACK: Christmas mull, Celery and peanut boats, Prune, almond and bacon rolls, Stilton dip with cheese sablées, Crudités

Prune, almond and bacon rolls

Makes 20

20 plump no-need-to-soak prunes, stoned

20 blanched whole almonds

20 streaky bacon rashers, rinded

Preparation time: *20 minutes*
Cooking time: *about 10 minutes*

1. Fill the cavity of each prune with an almond.
2. Lay the bacon rashers on a board and stretch them slightly with the back of a knife, then wrap one round each prune.
3. Arrange the prune, almond and bacon rolls in a foil-lined baking tin and cook under a moderate grill for 5–10 minutes, turning once, until the bacon is crispy. Serve hot, speared with cocktail sticks.

Celery and peanut boats

4 tablespoons crunchy peanut butter

25 g (1 oz) butter

salt

freshly ground black pepper

1 tablespoon finely chopped spring onions or chives

a good pinch of dried thyme

pinch of garlic salt (optional)

15 g (½ oz) fresh white breadcrumbs

a few drops of lemon juice

6 celery sticks, trimmed

paprika, to finish

Preparation time: *15 minutes, plus chilling.*

1. In a bowl, beat the peanut butter with the butter until smooth. Season well with salt and pepper and add the spring onions, herbs and garlic salt, if using. Stir in the breadcrumbs, adding enough lemon juice to give a spreading consistency.
2. Spoon the mixture into the cavity in the celery, then sprinkle lightly with paprika.
3. Cut the celery into 2.5 cm (1 inch) lengths and arrange on a plate. Chill in the refrigerator until ready to serve.

White wine cup

Makes about 3.75 litres (6½ pints)	900 ml (1½ pints) tonic water, well chilled or 450 ml (¾ pint) each tonic water and fizzy lemonade, well chilled
3 bottles dry white wine, well chilled	
½–¾ bottle dry sherry, well chilled	crushed ice
4–6 tablespoons Curaçao or Grand Marnier	a few cucumber slices
	1 orange, thinly sliced
	1 apple, cored and sliced

Preparation time: *15 minutes*

1. Combine all the ingredients in a large bowl. Chill in the refrigerator until required.
2. Put a handful of crushed ice in the base of serving jugs and pour over the wine cup. Add the cucumber, orange and apple slices and serve at once.

Smoked cod's roe pinwheels

100 g (4 oz) smoked cod's roe	1 tablespoon chopped fresh parsley (optional)
1–2 teaspoons lemon juice	1 small uncut brown loaf, crust removed
100 g (4 oz) softened butter	
freshly ground black pepper	parsley sprigs, to garnish

Preparation time: *about 25 minutes, plus chilling*

1. In a bowl, mash the cod's roe with the lemon juice with a fork, then beat in the butter until smooth. Season to taste with pepper and stir in the parsley, if using.
2. Cut the loaf lengthways into 4 thin slices.
3. Spread the bread slices with the smoked cod's roe mixture and roll up neatly beginning with a short end. Wrap the rolls tightly in cling film or non-stick silicone paper, screwing the ends together, and chill for at least 1 hour or overnight.
4. Cut the rolls crossways into thin slices and arrange on a plate. Garnish with parsley sprigs.

VARIATIONS:
Spread the bread with 1 × 40 g (1½ oz) can dressed crab mixed with 150 g (5 oz) softened butter; or 100 g (4 oz) smooth pâté mixed with 150 g (5 oz) softened butter.

Cheese and anchovy twists

100 g (4 oz) puff pastry made with 100 g (4 oz) plain flour (page 16) or 100 g (4 oz) shortcrust pastry made with 100 g (4 oz) plain flour (page 16)	2 cans anchovy fillets, soaked in milk for 5 minutes, then drained
	a little milk
	2 tablespoons grated Parmesan cheese

Preparation time: *about 15 minutes*
Cooking time: *about 15 minutes*
Oven: *220°C, 425°F, Gas Mark 7*

1. Roll out the pastry to a 30 cm (12 inch) square about 3 mm (⅛ inch) thick. Trim the edges neatly with a sharp knife. Cut the pastry into quarters then cut each quarter into strips 1–2 cm (½–¾ inch) wide.
2. Cut the anchovy fillets in half lengthways. Brush the strips with milk, then lay a piece of anchovy on each pastry strip. Sprinkle with the Parmesan cheese.
3. Give each strip one or two twists and lay on a baking sheet lined with non-stick silicone paper. Bake in a preheated hot oven for about 15 minutes or until lightly browned. Transfer to a wire rack and leave to cool completely, then store in an airtight container. Serve warm or cold.

Cocktail canapés

24 small biscuits	50 g (2 oz) cream cheese
softened butter, for spreading	50 g (2 oz) smoked salmon pieces
4 hard-boiled eggs	1 × 100 g (4 oz) can asparagus spears, drained
¼ cucumber, sliced	
50 g (2 oz) peeled prawns	

Preparation time: *45 minutes*

1. Spread 12 small biscuits with butter then top with a slice of hard boiled egg, half a slice of cucumber, a peeled prawn and sprig of parsley.
2. On 12 other biscuits, pipe 2 rows of cream cheese across the biscuits, place a small roll of smoked salmon in the centre of the cheese and top with an asparagus spear.

CLOCKWISE FROM FRONT : *Cheese and anchovy twists, Curry puffs with watercress dip, Smoked cod's roe pinwheels, Cocktail canapés*

Curry puffs with watercress

Makes about 25

½ recipe quantity choux pastry made with 50 g (2 oz) butter (page 18)

25 g (1 oz) butter or margarine

1 onion, peeled and finely chopped

2 teaspoons curry powder vegetable oil, for deep frying

SAUCE:

4 tablespoons thick mayonnaise

2 tablespoons plain unsweetened yogurt

1 bunch watercress, trimmed and finely chopped

grated rind of ½ lemon

Preparation time: *about 20 minutes*
Cooking time: *about 25 minutes*

1. Make the choux pastry as on page 18. Melt the butter in a small saucepan, add the onion and fry over a gentle heat for about 7 minutes, until lightly browned. Stir in the curry powder and allow to cool slightly, then beat into the choux paste.

2. Heat the oil to 180°–190°C (350–375°F) or until a cube of bread browns in 30 seconds.

3. Drop small teaspoons of the choux mixture into the oil, about 6 at a time. Fry for about 3–4 minutes, turning if necessary, until well puffed up and golden brown. Drain on paper towels and keep warm while frying the remainder in the same way.

4. Combine the sauce ingredients in a small bowl and stir well to mix. Garnish with a sprig of watercress, if liked. Stand the bowl containing the watercress dip on a large plate surrounded by the puffs speared with cocktail sticks, if liked.

Twelfth Night

Stilton Pâté with Pears

Paupiettes of Sole Bon Noël

Old English Raspberry Trifle

Stilton pâté with pears

Serves 6

225 g (8 oz) full fat soft cheese or curd cheese	freshly ground black pepper
2 tablespoons dry white wine	pinch of ground nutmeg
2 tablespoons top of the milk	3 ripe pears
175 g (6 oz Stilton, rind removed, finely grated	juice of 1 lemon
salt	1–2 bunches watercress, trimmed
	18 walnut halves
	lemon twists

Preparation time: *about 15 minutes, plus chilling time*

1. In a bowl beat the soft cheese with the wine and sufficient milk to give a smooth, creamy mixture. Stir in the Stilton and season to taste with salt, pepper and nutmeg.
2. Shape into a roll about 4 cm (1½ inches) in diameter and wrap in cling film, non-stick silicone paper or foil. Chill in the refrigerator for at least 1 hour or until required.
3. Just before serving, peel, core and slice each pear into 8 slices and dip the slices into the lemon juice to prevent discolouring. Arrange 4 pear slices on each of 6 small plates. Unwrap the Stilton pâté and cut into 12 even slices. Arrange 2 slices on each plate with the pears and garnish with watercress sprigs, walnut halves and lemon twists.
4. Serve with fingers of hot brown toast or crackers.
[F] Remove from the freezer 30 minutes before serving.

Paupiettes of sole bon Noël

Serves 6

6 large fillets of sole, about 225–300 g (8–10 oz) each, skinned	40 g (1½ oz) butter, diced
salt	200 ml (8 fl oz) dry white wine
freshly ground black pepper	1 tablespoon cornflour
1 × 350 g (12 oz) can asparagus spears, drained or 225 g (8 oz) frozen asparagus, thawed	150 ml (¼ pint) soured cream
175 g (6 oz) peeled prawns	1 egg yolk
	3 tablespoons dry white breadcrumbs
	6 unpeeled prawns, to garnish

Preparation time: *40 minutes*
Cooking time: *about 1 hour*
Oven: *190°C, 375°F, Gas Mark 5*

1. Lay the sole fillets on a board, skin side up, and season well with salt and pepper.
2. Lay the asparagus spears on the sole fillets, dividing them equally among the fillets, then scatter over about three-quarters of the prawns. Roll up the fillets from head to tail and place seam side down in a greased shallow baking dish.
3. Scatter over the remaining prawns and dot with the butter. Add the wine to the dish, cover with foil and cook in a preheated moderately hot oven for about 50 minutes or until cooked through.
4. Strain off the cooking liquid into a saucepan. Blend the cornflour with the soured cream and egg yolk and whisk into the pan. Bring to the boil, stirring continuously, then lower the heat and simmer for 2 minutes. Taste and adjust the seasoning and pour the sauce over the paupiettes of sole.
5. Sprinkle evenly with dry breadcrumbs and place under a moderate grill until lightly browned. Garnish with the whole prawns and serve at once, with braised celery and sauté potatoes.

CLOCKWISE FROM FRONT: *Stilton pâté with pears, Paupiettes of sole bon Noël, Old English raspberry trifle*

Old English raspberry trifle

Serves 6–8

1 × 20 cm (8 inch) Victoria sandwich cake or 6–8 trifle sponges	600 ml (1 pint) milk
	4 egg yolks
approx 75 g (3 oz) raspberry jam	4 tablespoons caster sugar
4 tablespoons sherry	a few drops of vanilla essence
225–350 g (8–12 oz) frozen raspberries, partly thawed	TOPPING:
CUSTARD:	300 ml (½ pint) double or whipping cream
2 tablespoons cornflour	walnut halves
	angelica

Preparation time: *about 40 minutes, plus chilling*
Cooking time: *about 5 minutes*

1. Split the cake in half and sandwich together with the jam. Cut into 2.5 cm (1 inch) cubes and place in a glass serving bowl; sprinkle with the sherry.
2. Arrange the raspberries over the cake and leave until almost completely thawed, so that the juices run down into the cake.
3. Make the custard: blend the cornflour with the milk in a bowl, then whisk in the egg yolks and strain into a saucepan. Add the sugar and bring slowly to the boil, stirring continuously. Cook until thickened, stirring, then remove from the heat and stir in the vanilla essence. Allow the custard to cool slightly, then pour over the raspberries and chill in the refrigerator until set.
4. Whip the cream until stiff and put into a piping bag fitted with a large star nozzle. Pipe a lattice or wheel design on top of the trifle. Decorate with walnuts and angelica and chill again in the refrigerator before serving.

Instant turkey hollandaise

Serves 4

225 g (8 oz) frozen broccoli spears

salt

8 slices cooked turkey meat, about 350 g (12 oz)

1 × 300 g (10 oz) can condensed chicken soup

2 tablespoons lemon juice

2–3 tablespoons dry white wine

4 tablespoons thick mayonnaise

freshly ground black pepper

25–40 g (1–1½ oz) fresh white breadcrumbs

25–40 g (1–1½ oz) mature Cheddar cheese, grated

Preparation time: *5–10 minutes*

Cooking time: *30 minutes*

Oven: *220°C, 425°F, Gas Mark 7*

1. Cook the broccoli in a saucepan of boiling salted water for 2–3 minutes, then drain and arrange in a greased shallow ovenproof dish.

2. Arrange the turkey slices over the broccoli.

3. Combine the chicken soup, lemon juice, wine and mayonnaise and season well with salt and pepper. Pour evenly over the turkey.

4. Mix the breadcrumbs with the cheese and sprinkle evenly over the surface of the dish.

5. Cook towards the top of a preheated hot oven for 25–30 minutes until bubbling and golden brown. Serve at once.

Turkey soup

Serves 10–12

1 turkey carcass	2 celery sticks, finely chopped
1 onion, peeled and quartered; 2 onions, peeled and finely chopped	1 tablespoon Worcestershire sauce
4 carrots, scraped and halved	25 g (1 oz) long-grain rice
1 bay leaf	salt
2.25 litres (4 pints) water	freshly ground black pepper
2 leeks, trimmed and finely chopped	50 g (2 oz) plain flour
225 g (8 oz) parsnips, peeled and finely chopped	50 g (2 oz) butter or margarine
	150 ml (¼ pint) single cream (optional)

Preparation time: *30 minutes*
Cooking time: *about 2½ hours*

1. Break up the carcass and put it into a large saucepan with the onion quarters, carrots, bay leaf and water. Bring up to the boil, remove any scum from the surface, cover and simmer for 1½ hours. Alternatively cook in a pressure cooker allowing 15 minutes on high.
2. Strain off the stock. [F] Reserve 2–2.25 litres (3½–4 pints). Strip off any turkey trimmings from the carcass and chop finely with the cooked carrots.
3. Place the carrots and turkey trimmings in a clean saucepan with the reserved stock, all the remaining vegetables, the Worcestershire sauce, rice and salt and pepper to taste. Bring to the boil, then lower the heat and simmer gently for 30 minutes, stirring occasionally.
4. Cream the flour and fat together and gradually whisk into the soup, whisking well between each addition. Return to the boil for 5 minutes. [F] Stir in the cream, if using. Taste and adjust seasoning and serve the soup in warmed soup bowls.

[F] The stock may be cooled and frozen for up to 2 months or the complete soup may also be frozen for up to 2 months.

VARIATIONS:
For a thicker, smoother soup, sieve, blend or purée in a food processor.

Turkey, ham and almond pie

Serves 4–5

40 g (1½ oz) butter or margarine	2 tablespoons soured cream or thick mayonnaise
25 g (1 oz) flaked almonds	100 g (4 oz) green or black grapes, halved and seeded
25 g (1 oz) plain flour	350 g (12 oz) cooked turkey meat, diced
150 ml (¼ pint) dry white wine	100 g (4 oz) cooked bacon or ham, diced
300 ml (½ pint) chicken stock or milk	50 g (2 oz) leftover stuffing, crumbled (optional)
salt	300 g (12 oz) shortcrust pastry made with 300 g (12 oz) plain flour (page 16)
freshly ground black pepper	beaten egg or milk, to glaze
½ teaspoon dried marjoram or oregano	

Preparation time: *30 minutes*
Cooking time: *50–60 minutes*
Oven: *220°C, 425°F, Gas Mark 7*
then: *180°C, 350°F, Gas Mark 4*

1. Melt the butter in a frying pan, add the almonds and fry over a moderate heat until light brown. Stir in the flour, remove from the heat and stir until well blended. Gradually stir in the wine and stock and bring to the boil, then lower the heat and simmer for 1–2 minutes. Season well with salt and pepper, add the herbs and stir in the cream. Turn into a large bowl. Mix in the grapes, turkey and ham, cover and leave to cool.
2. Roll out about two-thirds of the pastry and use to line a shallow 23 cm (9 inch) pie dish. Spoon in the filling and sprinkle with the stuffing, if using.
3. Roll out the remaining pastry slightly larger than the top of the pie dish. Cut off a pastry strip 2.5 cm (1 inch) wide and fit on to the dampened rim of the pie dish. Brush the pastry strip with water, then cover with the lid and press the edges firmly together. Trim and crimp the edge.
4. Roll out the pastry trimmings and cut out leaves. Make a small hole in the top of the pie and decorate round the hole with the pastry leaves. Brush the leaves with beaten egg.
5. Bake the pie in a preheated hot oven for 20 minutes. Reduce the oven temperature to moderate and bake for a further 20–30 minutes or until the pastry is golden brown and cooked through. Serve hot or cold. [F]

[F] Thaw the pie and reheat in a 180°C, 350°F, Gas Mark 4 oven for about 30 minutes until piping hot; cover with foil if overbrowning.

LEFT: Instant turkey hollandaise RIGHT: Turkey soup

Turkey and spinach pancakes

Serves 4

PANCAKE BATTER:
100 g (4 oz) plain flour
pinch of salt
2 eggs
275 ml (scant ½ pint) milk
lard, for frying
FILLING:
50 g (2 oz) butter or margarine
1 onion, peeled and chopped
2 tablespoons plain flour
300 ml (½ pint) milk or chicken stock
salt
freshly ground black pepper
¼ teaspoon ground nutmeg

225 g (8 oz) frozen chopped spinach, cooked and drained
300 g (10 oz) cooked turkey meat, chopped
40 g (1½ oz) shelled walnuts, chopped (optional)
SAUCE:
40 g (1½ oz) butter or margarine
40 g (1½ oz) plain flour
300 ml (½ pint) cider
150 ml (¼ pint) milk
1 teaspoon made English mustard
40 g (1½ oz) Cheddar cheese, grated

Preparation time: *50 minutes*
Cooking time: *30–40 minutes*
Oven: *220°C, 425°F, Gas Mark 7*

1. Make the pancakes: sift the flour with the salt into a mixing bowl. Make a well in the centre, add the eggs and gradually add the milk, drawing the flour into the liquid with a wooden spoon and beating well until smooth.
2. Grease a small frying pan with lard, drain off the excess and use the batter to make 8 pancakes in the usual way. Stack with greaseproof paper between each one.
3. Make the filling: melt the butter in a saucepan, add the onion and fry over a gentle heat for 5 minutes until soft. Stir in the flour, cook for 1 minute, then remove from the heat and gradually stir in the milk. Bring to the boil, then lower the heat and simmer for 1–2 minutes, stirring frequently. Season well with salt, pepper and nutmeg.
4. Add the spinach to the sauce with the turkey meat and walnuts, if using.
5. Divide the mixture between the pancakes, roll up and place seam side down in a greased ovenproof dish.
6. Make the sauce: melt the butter in a saucepan, stir in the flour and cook for 1 minute. Remove from the heat and gradually stir in the cider and milk. Bring to the boil, then lower the heat and simmer for 1 minute, stirring continuously. Season well and stir in the mustard.
7. Pour the sauce over the pancakes and sprinkle with the cheese. [F] Bake in a preheated hot oven for 15–20 minutes or until well browned. Serve at once.

[A] The pancakes may be made 2–3 days in advance. The filling may be made 24 hours in advance.
[F] Thaw and cook in a fairly hot oven (200°C, 400°F, Gas Mark 6) for about 40 minutes.

Raised turkey pie

Serves 8

225 g (8 oz) pie veal or lean pork, minced
225 g (8 oz) cooked ham, minced
1 small onion, peeled
½ teaspoon ground coriander seeds
salt
freshly ground black pepper
450 g (1 lb) plain flour

100 g (4 oz) lard
150 ml (¼ pint) water
4 tablespoons milk
350 g (12 oz) cooked turkey meat, finely chopped
beaten egg, to glaze
2 teaspoons powdered gelatine
150 ml (¼ pint) hot chicken stock
150 ml (¼ pint) dry cider

Preparation time: *about 45 minutes*
Cooking time: *about 2 hours*
Oven: *200°C, 400°F, Gas Mark 6*
then: *160°C, 325°F, Gas Mark 3*

1. Combine the veal, ham, onion and coriander in a bowl and season well with salt and pepper.
2. Make the pastry: sift the flour with 1 teaspoon salt into a mixing bowl. Put the lard with the water and milk in a saucepan, stir until the lard is melted and then bring up to the boil. Add all at once to the flour and work to form a pliable dough. Knead lightly.
3. Roll out three-quarters of the pastry and use to line a greased raised pie mould, 18–20 cm (7–8 inch) round or square loose-based cake tin or a 1 kg (2 lb) loaf tin.
4. Put half the minced veal mixture in the base of the pie mould, cover with chopped turkey and then with the remaining minced veal mixture.
5. Roll out the remaining pastry for a lid, damp the pastry edges, cover with the lid and press well together. Trim the edges and crimp and make a hole in the centre. Brush all over with beaten egg.
6. Roll out the pastry trimmings and cut out leaves. Use to decorate around the central hole and brush the leaves with beaten egg.
7. Bake in a preheated moderately hot oven for 30 minutes. Reduce the oven temperature and bake for a further 1¼–1½ hours. (Cover the pie with greaseproof paper when sufficiently browned.)
8. Dissolve the gelatine in the stock, season well with salt and pepper and add the cider. As the pie cools pour the stock into the pie through a funnel inserted in the central hole, tilting the pie to ensure that the stock is evenly distributed inside the pie.
9. Cool, then chill overnight until firm, before removing from the tin. Serve cut into slices with a selection of salads.

FRONT: Turkey and spinach pancakes BACK: Raised turkey pie

Potted turkey

Serves 4–6

225 g (8 oz) cooked turkey meat, minced twice	salt
100 g (4 oz) butter	freshly ground black pepper
1 onion, peeled and very finely chopped	pinch of ground nutmeg
1–2 cloves garlic, peeled and crushed	pinch of dried thyme (optional)
2 tablespoons sherry or port	TO GARNISH:
a little stock	lettuce leaves
	watercress
	tomatoes

Preparation time: *30 minutes*
Cooking time: *5 minutes*

Potted turkey is ideal to serve as a starter, with toast, as a snack, or as a filling for sandwiches. It is also excellent served on tiny squares of fried bread as a cocktail snack. It will keep for 2–3 days in the refrigerator or for up to 2 months in the freezer.

1. Melt half the butter in a frying pan, add the onion and fry over a gentle heat for about 5 minutes until soft but not coloured.
2. Stir in the turkey meat followed by the sherry and sufficient stock just to moisten. Season well with salt and pepper and add the nutmeg and thyme.
3. Pack the mixture into a lightly greased dish and level the top. Chill in the refrigerator until firm.
4. Melt the remaining butter in a small saucepan and pour a thin layer over the turkey. Chill until required.

Alternative Christmas

Romantic Christmas

Smoked Salmon and Prawn Salad

Cranberry Duck with Pastry Tartlets

Christmas Pancake Parcels
with Brandy Sauce

Smoked salmon and prawn salad

Serves 2	1 teaspoon lemon juice
3 tablespoons thick mayonnaise	75–100 g (3–4 oz) peeled prawns
½ teaspoon creamed horseradish	2 slices smoked salmon 75–100 g (3–4 oz)
1 teaspoon capers, chopped	lettuce leaves
	TO GARNISH:
1 teaspoon chopped fresh parsley	cucumber slices
	lemon slices

Preparation time: *about 15 minutes*

1. In a bowl combine the mayonnaise, horseradish, capers, parsley and lemon juice. Add the prawns and turn to coat thoroughly.
2. Lay the salmon slices on a board and divide the prawn mixture equally between them. Roll up carefully.
3. Arrange lettuce leaves on 2 small plates and place the salmon rolls on top. Garnish with cucumber and lemon slices and serve with brown bread and butter.

Cranberry duck

Serves 2	grated rind of ½ orange
2–2.75 kg (4½–6 lb) oven-ready duck	juice of 1 orange
	juice of 1 lemon
salt	freshly ground black pepper
150 ml (¼ pint) beef stock	
2–3 tablespoons cranberry sauce	1½ teaspoons cornflour
	orange segments, to garnish
2–3 tablespoons port	

Preparation time: *15 minutes*
Cooking time: *1¼–1½ hours*
Oven: 220°C, 425°F. Gas Mark 7

1. Prick the duck all over with a fork and place in a roasting tin. Sprinkle lightly with salt.
2. Roast in a preheated hot oven for about 1 hour or until cooked through, basting once during cooking.
3. Remove the duck to a serving dish and keep warm. Drain off all the fat from the tin, leaving just the juices. Combine the stock, cranberry sauce, port, orange rind and juice and lemon juice and pour into the tin. Bring to the boil, stirring frequently with a wooden spoon and scraping the base and sides of the tin to remove the sediment. Simmer for 2–3 minutes.
4. Blend the cornflour with a little cold water to make a smooth paste. Stir into the tin and simmer for a further 2–3 minutes until thickened. Season to taste with salt and pepper and pour into a warmed sauce boat.
6. Garnish the duck with orange segments and Pastry tartlets filled with minted peas (see below) and serve with the sauce handed separately. Roast potatoes and steamed broccoli spears would also make good accompaniments.

Pastry tartlets

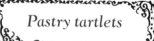

Roll out about 100 g (4 oz) shortcrust pastry made with 100 g (4 oz) plain flour (page 16), and use a fluted round biscuit cutter to cut circles to line six patty tins. Bake blind in a hot oven (200°C, 400°F, Gas Mark 6) for 10–15 minutes. Remove the paper and beans and return the pastry cases to the oven for a few minutes to dry out. Transfer to a wire rack and leave to cool completely. These may be made 2 or 3 days in advance and stored in an airtight container.
To serve: reheat the tartlets. Cook 100–175 g (4–6 oz) frozen peas, drain and keep warm. Mix 1 teaspoon concentrated mint sauce into 2–3 tablespoons soured cream with a pinch of sugar to taste. Fill the tartlets with hot peas and top each with a little cream dressing.

Christmas pancake parcels

Serves 2

BATTER:
50 g (2 oz) plain flour
pinch of salt
1 egg
150 ml (¼ pint) milk
lard or butter, for frying
FILLING:
225 g (8 oz) cooking apples
about 2 tablespoons cider

soft light brown sugar or honey, to taste
2 tablespoons mincemeat
¼–½ teaspoon mixed spice
40 g (1½ oz) butter or margarine, for frying
brandy sauce (see below)
orange or lemon slices, to decorate

Preparation time: *about 30 minutes*
Cooking time: *about 25 minutes*

1. Make the pancakes: sift the flour with the salt into a mixing bowl. Make a well in the centre, add the egg and a little of the milk and gradually beat in the flour using a wooden spoon, adding the rest of the milk a little at a time to make a smooth batter.

2. Use the batter to make 4 pancakes in a small frying pan in the usual way.

3. Make the filling: peel, core and slice the apples and cook in a saucepan with the cider over a gentle heat until tender. Drain off any surplus liquid then add sugar to taste and stir in the mincemeat and spice.

4. Divide the filling between the pancakes and fold up into parcels to enclose the filling completely. Chill in the refrigerator until ready to serve.

5. Melt the butter in a frying pan and when hot add the pancake parcels and fry over a moderately high heat until well browned and crisp. Drain on paper towels and keep warm. Decorate with orange or lemon slices and serve with Brandy sauce.

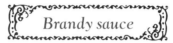

Brandy sauce

1 teaspoon cornflour
150 ml (¼ pint) milk

1 egg yolk
1 tablespoon sugar
10 g (¼ oz) butter
2–3 tablespoons brandy

Preparation time: *5 minutes*
Cooking time: *5 minutes*

1. Blend the cornflour with the milk in a bowl, then stir in the egg yolk and sugar. Put into a saucepan and bring up to the boil, stirring continuously, until slightly thickened.

2. Stir in the butter and brandy to taste, reheat and serve hot with the pancake parcels.

CLOCKWISE FROM FRONT: *Cranberry duck with Pastry tartlets, Smoked salmon and prawn salad, Cranberry sauce*

Vegetarian Christmas

Courgette Ratatouille

Pine Nut Roast

Spicy Tomato Sauce

Parsnip Duchesse Potatoes

Red Fruit Salad with
Fluffy Yogurt (page 59)

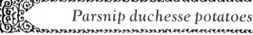

Parsnip duchesse potatoes

Serves 6	salt
750 g (1½ lb) parsnips, peeled and cut into equal pieces	freshly ground black pepper
	pinch of ground nutmeg
750 g (1½ lb) potatoes, peeled	1 egg

Preparation time: *20 minutes*
Cooking time: *about 50 minutes*
Oven: *200°C, 400°F, Gas Mark 6*

1. Cook the parsnips and potatoes in separate saucepans of boiling salted water for about 20 minutes, until tender. Drain very thoroughly.
2. Mash the parsnips and potatoes together and process in a food processor until smooth, then rub through a sieve. Turn into a bowl, season well with salt and pepper and beat in the nutmeg and egg.
3. Put the mixture into a piping bag fitted with a large star nozzle and pipe large whirls of the mixture on to a greased baking sheet. **A**
4. Bake in a preheated hot oven for about 25 minutes or until lightly browned. Serve hot.

A These may be prepared earlier in the day. If cooking from cold increase the cooking time by about 5 minutes.

Courgette ratatouille

Serves 6	450 g (1 lb) courgettes, trimmed and sliced
4 tablespoons olive oil	salt
2 large onions, peeled and sliced	freshly ground black pepper
1–2 cloves garlic, peeled and crushed	1–2 tablespoons white wine or wine vinegar
1–2 red peppers, cored, seeded and sliced	chopped fresh parsley
1 green pepper, cored, seeded and sliced	

Preparation time: *15 minutes*
Cooking time: *20 minutes*

1. Heat the oil in a frying pan, add the onions and garlic and fry over a gentle heat for 5 minutes until soft and lightly coloured. Add the peppers and fry for a further 3–4 minutes or until the peppers are soft. Add the courgettes and stir well to mix.
2. Season well with salt and pepper, add the wine and cook over a gentle heat for about 5 minutes, stirring frequently. (The courgettes should still be slightly crisp.) Taste and adjust the seasoning.
3. Sprinkle the ratatouille with chopped parsley and serve hot or cold, with wholemeal or rye bread.

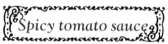
Spicy tomato sauce

250 ml (8 fl oz) tomato ketchup	salt
	freshly ground black pepper
250 ml (9 fl oz) red wine	1–2 cloves garlic, peeled and crushed

Preparation time: *5 minutes*
Cooking time: *10 minutes*

Put the ketchup and the wine into a saucepan with salt, freshly ground black pepper and garlic to taste. Bring to the boil and simmer, uncovered, for about 10 minutes until the sauce is thick enough to coat the back of a spoon. Taste and adjust the seasoning and serve with the Pine nut roast.

LEFT TO RIGHT: Parsnip duchesse potatoes, Pine nut roast with Spicy tomato sauce, Courgette ratatouille

Pine nut roast

Serves 6

40 g (1½ oz) butter or margarine	freshly grated nutmeg
2–3 tablespoons dried breadcrumbs	STUFFING:
1 onion, peeled and chopped	100 g (4 oz) butter, softened
50 g (2 oz) pine nuts	grated rind and juice of ½ lemon
100 g (4 oz) cashew nuts, grated or very finely chopped	½ teaspoon dried thyme
50 g (2 oz) ground almonds	4 tablespoons chopped fresh parsley
100 g (4 oz) fresh brown or white breadcrumbs	1 clove garlic, peeled and crushed
4 tablespoons milk	100 g (4 oz) fresh brown breadcrumbs
2 eggs, beaten	TO GARNISH:
salt	2 tablespoons pine nuts, toasted
freshly ground black pepper	lemon slices
	parsley sprigs

Preparation time: *30 minutes*
Cooking time: *about 1 hour*
Oven: *180°C, 350°F, Gas Mark 4*

1. Line a 23 × 12.5 × 7.5 cm (9 × 5 × 3 inch) loaf tin with non-stick silicone paper. Grease the paper with 15 g (½ oz) of the butter, then coat with the dried breadcrumbs.

2. Melt the remaining butter in a frying pan, add the onion and fry over a gentle heat for about 7 minutes until soft and lightly browned. Turn into a bowl and add the nuts, breadcrumbs, milk, eggs and salt, pepper and nutmeg to taste. Stir well to mix.

3. Make the stuffing: cream the butter in a bowl, then gradually work in all the other ingredients until thoroughly blended.

4. Spoon half the nut mixture into the base of the prepared tin. Cover with the stuffing then with the remaining nuts. Smooth the surface and cover with a piece of buttered foil.

5. Bake in a preheated moderate oven for 1 hour. Remove the foil and return to the oven for 5–10 minutes if necessary to brown. Remove from the oven and leave to stand in the tin for 5 minutes.

6. Turn out very carefully on to a serving dish and gently pull off the paper. Sprinkle the toasted pine nuts over the top and garnish with lemon slices and parsley sprigs.

7. Serve the Pine nut roast with Parsnip duchesse potatoes, Brussels sprouts and leeks au gratin accompanied by Spicy tomato sauce or cranberry sauce.

Fishy Christmas

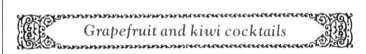

Grapefruit and Kiwi Cocktails

Salmon en Croûte

Hollandaise Sauce

Soufflé Olivia with Almond Tuiles

Grapefruit and kiwi cocktails

Serves 6	6–8 tablespoons medium
3 large or 6 small	sherry or madeira
grapefruit, halved	4–6 tablespoons demerara
4–5 kiwi fruit, peeled and	sugar
thinly sliced	

Preparation time: *20 minutes*

1. Using a grapefruit knife, carefully remove the segments from each grapefruit half. Discard any pith and cut up the segments.
2. Line the base and sides of the grapefruit shells with the kiwi fruit slices. Spoon the pieces of grapefruit into the centre, and sprinkle with sherry and sugar.
3. Chill in the refrigerator for 1 hour before serving.

Salmon en croûte

Serves 6	HOLLANDAISE SAUCE:
1.5 kg (3–3½ lb) salmon or	6 tablespoons white wine
salmon trout, cleaned and	vinegar
head removed, divided into	3 tablespoons water
2 fillets and skinned	10 black peppercorns,
juice of 1 lemon	crushed
salt	6 egg yolks
freshly ground black	175–300 g (6–10 oz) butter,
pepper	softened
50 g (2 oz) butter, softened	about 2 teaspoons lemon
1 teaspoon dried dillweed	juice
450 g (1 lb) puff pastry	TO GARNISH:
(page 16)	lemon slices
beaten egg, to glaze	cucumber sticks
	parsley sprigs

Preparation time: *45 minutes*
Cooking time: *about 50 minutes*
Oven: *200°C, 425°F, Gas Mark 7*
then: *190°C, 375°F, Gas Mark 5*

1. Rub the salmon fillets all over with lemon juice and season lightly with salt and pepper.
2. Lay one fillet on a board and spread with the butter, then sprinkle with the dillweed and cover with the second fillet to reshape the fish.
3. Roll out about three-quarters of the pastry thinly and use to enclose the fish, keeping to the shape as much as possible and sealing the edges well with beaten egg.
4. Place the salmon on a greased baking sheet and brush all over with beaten egg. Roll out the remaining pastry with the trimmings and use to cut into 'scales'. Arrange these all over the fish to represent scales from the head to the tail. Cut out a slightly enlarged pastry tail and an eye for the head. Brush the scales and tail with beaten egg.
5. Bake in a preheated hot oven for about 30 minutes. Reduce the oven temperature and bake for a further 20 minutes or until golden brown. (Cover with a sheet of greaseproof paper when sufficiently browned.)
6. Make the Hollandaise sauce: put the vinegar, water and peppercorns into a saucepan and boil hard until reduced by half. Strain into the top of a double saucepan or a heatproof bowl and whisk in the egg yolks. Cook over very gently simmering water until thick, stirring continuously. Whisk in the butter, a knob at a time, until the sauce is smooth, then season to taste with salt, pepper and lemon juice. Cover and keep warm.
7. Garnish the salmon with lemon and cucumber slices and parsley sprigs. Serve hot with new potatoes, a mixture of cooked peas, diced carrots and celery, and a salad, with the Hollandaise sauce handed separately in a warmed sauce boat.

Soufflé Olivia

Serves 8	3 tablespoons milk
2 tablespoons instant coffee (powder or granules)	40 g (1½ oz) flaked almonds, toasted
3 tablespoons boiling water	75 g (3 oz) plain dark chocolate, coarsely grated
4 eggs, separated	ALMOND TUILES:
175 g (6 oz) caster sugar	1 egg white
15 g (½ oz) packet powdered gelatine	50 g (2 oz) caster sugar
2 tablespoons coffee liqueur or rum	25 g (1 oz) plain flour, sifted
150 ml (¼ pint) double cream	25 g (1 oz) flaked almonds
	25 g (1 oz) butter, melted

Preparation time: *40 minutes*
Cooking time: *20 minutes*
Oven: *190°C, 375°F, Gas Mark 5*

1. Dissolve the coffee in the boiling water and leave to cool a little.
2. Put the egg yolks, sugar and dissolved coffee into a bowl and whisk until very thick and pale in colour and the whisk leaves a heavy trail when lifted.
3. Dissolve the gelatine in a small basin with the liqueur or rum and 1 tablespoon water over a pan of hot water. Cool slightly.
4. Whisk the egg whites until very stiff and whip the cream and milk together until thick but not too stiff.
5. Roughly break up the almonds and mix with the chocolate.
6. Mix the dissolved gelatine evenly into the coffee mixture then fold in the cream followed by the egg whites.
7. Pour a quarter of the soufflé into a glass or other serving bowl and sprinkle with some of the chocolate and nuts. Cover with the remainder of the soufflé and sprinkle with an even layer of the chocolate mixture. Chill until firm. [F]
8. For the tuiles: line 2 baking sheets with non-stick baking paper and grease several cream horn tins. Whisk the egg white until very stiff then gently fold in the sugar, flour and almonds. Finally fold in the butter. Put teaspoons of the mixture on the baking sheets and spread out thinly. Bake in a moderately hot oven for 8–10 minutes or until browned around the edges and a pale brown in the centre. Cool slightly then remove with a palette knife and wind quickly around the horn tins. Cool on a wire rack and slip out the tins as soon as they are firm. When cold store in an airtight container.

[F] The soufflé may be frozen for up to 3 months. Thaw out in a cool place allowing up to 12 hours or overnight.

LEFT TO RIGHT: Grapefruit and kiwi cocktails, Soufflé Olivia, Salmon en croûte with Hollandaise sauce, Almond tuiles

Partridges for Christmas

Green Soup

Roast Partridges with Crunchy Stuffing Balls

Chocolate Chestnut Gâteau

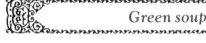

Green soup

Serves 6	1 tablespoon lemon juice
50 g (2 oz) butter or margarine	1 teaspoon Worcestershire sauce
2 large leeks, about 400 g (14 oz) trimmed and sliced	pinch of ground mace
	salt
350 g (12 oz) Brussels sprouts, trimmed and shredded	freshly ground black pepper
	300 ml (½ pint) milk or half milk and half single cream
1 litre (1¾ pint) chicken stock	fried onion rings, to garnish

Preparation time: *20 minutes*
Cooking time: *about 45 minutes*

1. Melt the butter in a saucepan, add the leeks and fry over a gentle heat for 5 minutes, stirring occasionally.
2. Add the Brussels sprouts, stir well, then add the stock, lemon juice, Worcestershire sauce, mace and salt and pepper and bring to the boil.
3. Cover the pan and simmer for 20–25 minutes or until the vegetables are very tender. Cool slightly, then purée in a food processor or blender, or pass through a sieve.
4. Return the soup to the rinsed out pan with the milk. Return to the boil, taste and adjust the seasoning. Serve the soup in warmed individual soup bowls, garnished with fried onion rings and accompanied by toasted slices of French bread.

Roast partridges with crunchy stuffing balls

Serves 6	25 g (1 oz) butter or margarine
6 oven-ready partridges	
salt	75 g (3 oz) fresh white breadcrumbs
freshly ground black pepper	
	grated rind of ½ lemon
12 rashers streaky bacon, rinded	40 g (1½ oz) cashew nuts, chopped
6 lemon wedges	1 dessert apple, cored and coarsely grated
50 g (2 oz) butter	
2 tablespoons vegetable oil	2 tablespoons chopped fresh parsley
300 ml (½ pint) red wine	
6 circles of bread	good pinch of dried thyme
3 tablespoons coarse cut orange marmalade	1 egg, beaten
	TO GARNISH:
1–2 tablespoons lemon juice	small bunch of green grapes
STUFFING BALLS:	watercress sprigs
1 onion, peeled and chopped	

Preparation time: *about 40 minutes*
Cooking time: *about 1¼ hours*
Oven: *220°C, 425°F, Gas Mark 7*

1. Wipe the partridges, season well with salt and pepper and lay 2 rashers of bacon over each bird. Put a lemon wedge in the cavity of each and place the partridges in a large roasting tin. Rub all over with the butter and pour over the oil.
2. Roast in a preheated hot oven for 20 minutes, basting once. Bring the wine to the boil, pour over the partridges and cook for a further 30 minutes or until tender, basting once or twice with the wine.
3. Make the stuffing balls: melt the butter in a small saucepan, add the onion and fry over a gentle heat for 5 minutes, until soft and lightly coloured. Add the breadcrumbs, lemon rind, cashew nuts, apple, salt and pepper, parsley and thyme and stir in the egg to bind. Form the mixture into 12 balls, place on a greased baking sheet and cook in the oven under the partridges for 30 minutes.
4. Toast or fry the bread circles and place on a serving dish; place a partridge on each and keep warm.
5. Drain off the excess fat from the roasting tin, stir the marmalade into the juices and simmer gently for about 5 minutes or until syrupy. Taste and adjust the seasoning and sharpen with lemon juice if necessary.
6. Serve the partridges on the fried bread, surrounded with stuffing balls and garnished with small bunches of grapes and watercress sprigs, accompanied by new potatoes and French beans and the sauce, handed separately in a warmed sauce boat.

Chocolate chestnut gâteau

Serves 8	3 tablespoons rum
CAKE:	1 × 250 g (8½ oz) can
3 eggs	sweetened chestnut purée
120 g (4½ oz) caster sugar	300 ml (½ pint) whipping
75 g (3 oz) plain flour	cream
15 g (½ oz) cocoa powder	100 g (4 oz) plain dark
FILLING:	chocolate, coarsely grated
crème patissière (see	a few marzipan holly leaves
Shortbread meringue	and berries, to decorate
gâteau, page 56)	(page 14)

Preparation time: *about 40 minutes*
Cooking time: *35–40 minutes*
Oven: *190°C, 375°F, Gas Mark 5*

1. Grease a 20–22 cm (8–8½ inch) round cake tin and line with greased greaseproof paper. Put the eggs and sugar into a large bowl and whisk with an electric hand-held whisk until the mixture is thick and pale and the whisk leaves a heavy trail when lifted.

CLOCKWISE FROM THE FRONT: *Roast partridges with crunchy stuffing balls, Green soup, Chocolate chestnut gâteau*

2. Sift the flour and cocoa together twice and fold lightly and evenly through the egg mixture, using a large metal spoon. Pour the mixture into the prepared tin and bake in a preheated oven for about 35 minutes or until firm. Turn out on to a wire rack and leave to cool.
3. Make the crème patissière and leave to cool.
4. Split the cake horizontally into three layers and place the bottom layer on a serving dish. Spread with just over half the crème patissière and cover with the middle layer of cake; sprinkle with rum.
5. Beat half the chestnut spread into the remaining crème patissière and spread over the second layer of cake. Place the remaining layer on top.
6. Whip the cream and use about two-thirds to spread over the top and sides of the cake. Press the grated chocolate around the sides of the cake.
7. Put the remaining purée into a piping bag with a medium star nozzle and pipe a lacy pattern over the top.
8. Pipe the edge of the cake with whirls of cream, using a large star nozzle. Decorate with holly leaves and berries. Chill for at least 30 minutes before serving.

Stand-up Christmas

Egg and Tuna Mayonnaise
Pheasants in Red Wine with Chestnuts
Scalloped Potatoes
Tangy Red Cabbage
Shortbread Meringue
Gâteau
Choc au Rhum
Mousse

Egg and tuna mayonnaise

Serves 10

10 hard-boiled eggs, shelled	freshly ground black pepper
crisp lettuce leaves	approx 300 ml (½ pint) olive oil
1–2 cans anchovy fillets in oil, drained and roughly chopped	4–6 tablespoons mayonnaise
2 × 200 g (7 oz) cans tuna fish, drained and flaked	1 × 200 g (7 oz) can pimientos, drained and cut into strips
4 tablespoons lemon juice	watercress sprigs, to garnish
4 egg yolks	

Preparation time: *about 40 minutes*

1. Halve the eggs lengthways and place 2 halves cut side down on lettuce leaves on small plates or saucers.
2. Put the anchovies and tuna fish with the lemon juice into a food processor or blender and process until smooth.
3. Add the egg yolks, plenty of pepper and 4 tablespoons of the oil and process again until smooth. Gradually add the oil, with the motor running, until the sauce is of a thick coating consistency. Taste and adjust the seasoning and beat in the mayonnaise.
4. Spoon the tuna sauce over the eggs to coat completely. Garnish with pimiento strips, arranged in a lattice pattern over the eggs, and watercress sprigs. Serve with melba toast or crispbread and butter.

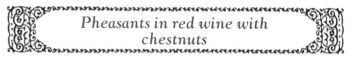

Pheasants in red wine with chestnuts

Serves 10

	STUFFING BALLS:
4 oven-ready pheasants	2 onions, peeled and very finely chopped
salt	
freshly ground black pepper	175 g (6 oz) celery, very finely chopped
3 tablespoons oil or dripping	50 g (2 oz) butter or margarine
2 large onions, peeled and sliced	2 tablespoons chopped fresh parsley
2 tablespoons plain flour	2 teaspoons dried thyme
450 ml (¾ pint) red wine	350 g (12 oz) fresh white breadcrumbs
450 ml (¾ pint) beef stock	
1 tablespoon black treacle	2 eggs, beaten
3–4 tablespoons brandy (optional)	a little lemon juice (optional)
1 bay leaf	parsley sprigs, to garnish
1 × 440 g (15½ oz) can whole peeled chestnuts, drained	

Preparation time: *about 40 minutes*
Cooking time: *about 1 ¾ hours*
Oven: *180°C, 350°F, Gas Mark 4*

1. Wipe the pheasants inside and out and season well with salt and pepper. Heat the oil in a large frying pan, add the pheasants one at a time and fry, turning, to brown all over. Transfer to a large roasting tin.
2. Add the onions to the pan and fry over a gentle heat for about 7 minutes until lightly browned. Sprinkle in the flour and cook for 1–2 minutes. Gradually stir in the wine and stock and bring to the boil. Stir in the treacle and brandy if using, season well with salt and pepper and add the bay leaf. Simmer for 2 minutes.
3. Add the chestnuts and pour the contents of the pan over the pheasants. Cover with foil and cook in a preheated moderate oven for about 1¼ hours or until tender and cooked thoroughly.
4. Meanwhile make the stuffing balls: melt the butter in a frying pan, add the onion and celery and fry over a gentle heat until soft. Turn into a bowl, season well with salt and pepper and add the herbs. Add the breadcrumbs and stir in the eggs to bind, with a little lemon juice if using. Form the mixture into 20 balls.
5. Arrange the stuffing balls in a greased tin and cook above the pheasants for the last 30 minutes of cooking time.
6. Transfer the pheasants to a large warmed serving dish. Garnish with the stuffing balls and parsley sprigs. Discard the bay leaf from the tin and pour the juices with the onions and chestnuts into heated sauce boats. Hand separately with the carved pheasants.

Scallopped potatoes

Serves 10

1.75 kg (4 lb) potatoes, peeled and thinly sliced	freshly ground black pepper
3 onions, peeled and thinly sliced	300 ml (½ pint) beef stock
salt	25 g (1 oz) butter, melted
	2 tablespoons fresh chopped parsley

Preparation time: *20 minutes*
Cooking time: *about 2 hours*
Oven: *180°C, 350°F, Gas Mark 4*

1. Make layers of the potatoes and onions in a well-greased ovenproof dish and season with salt and pepper.
2. Bring the stock to the boil and pour over the potatoes, then brush liberally with the melted butter.
3. Cover with foil and cook in a preheated moderate oven for 1½ hours. Remove the foil and cook for a further 30 minutes or until cooked through and lightly browned.
4. Place under a moderate grill until the potatoes are well browned and crispy on top. Sprinkle with parsley and serve hot.

LEFT TO RIGHT: Pheasants in red wine with chestnuts, Tangy red cabbage, Scalloped potatoes

Tangy red cabbage

Serves 10

2 tablespoons vegetable oil or dripping

1 large onion, peeled and thinly sliced

1.5 kg (3 lb) red cabbage, finely shredded

1 large cooking apple, peeled, cored and chopped

4 tablespoons red wine vinegar

3–4 tablespoons water

3 tablespoons soft light brown sugar

salt

freshly ground black pepper

Preparation time: *15 minutes*
Cooking time: *about 1¼ hours*

1. Heat the oil in a large saucepan, add the onion and fry over a gentle heat for about 5 minutes until soft and lightly coloured.
2. Add the cabbage, apple, vinegar and water to the pan. Stir well to mix and cook gently, stirring frequently, until beginning to soften. Add the sugar and season with salt and pepper. Mix well. Cover and simmer for 30 minutes, stirring from time to time.
3. Add 2–3 tablespoons water if the pan shows signs of drying out and cook for a further 30 minutes. Taste and adjust the seasoning and transfer to a warmed serving dish.

Variation: the cabbage may be transferred to a casserole in stage 2 and cooked in a moderate oven (180°C, 350°F, Gas Mark 4) for 1 hour.

Shortbread meringue gâteau

Serves 8–10

MERINGUE:

2 egg whites

50 g (2 oz) caster sugar

50 g (2 oz) soft light brown sugar

SHORTBREAD:

125 g (5 oz) plain flour

25 g (1 oz) custard powder

100 g (4 oz) butter

50 g (2 oz) demerara sugar

CRÈME PATISSIÈRE:

2 egg yolks

50 g (2 oz) caster sugar

20 g (¾ oz) plain flour

15 g (½ oz) cornflour

300 ml (½ pint) milk

a few drops of vanilla essence

10 g (¼ oz) butter

FILLING:

450 g (1 lb) fresh apricots or 2 × 425 g (15 oz) cans apricot halves, drained

300 ml (½ pint) double or whipping cream

angelica

Preparation time: *about 45 minutes*
Cooking time: *about 2¾ hours*
Oven: *110°C, 225°F, Gas Mark ¼*
then: *180°C, 350°F, Gas Mark 4*

Everything can be prepared in advance for this dessert but it should not be assembled more than 2 hours before serving.

1. Make the meringue: whisk the egg whites until very stiff, sift the sugars together twice, then whisk into the egg whites, a little at a time, making sure the meringue is stiff again before the next addition.
2. Draw a 22–23 cm (8½–9 inch) circle on a piece of non-stick silicone paper and place on a baking sheet. Spread or pipe the meringue to cover the circle. Bake in a preheated very cool oven for about 2 hours or until crisp and dry. Remove from the oven and leave to cool on the paper.
3. Make the shortbread: sift the flour with the custard powder into a bowl, add the butter and sugar and work together with the hands to make a smooth dough. Roll out a quarter of the dough on a lightly floured board or work surface and cut into 10 × 4 cm (1½ inch) circles, using a fluted cutter. Place on a baking sheet lined with non-stick silicone paper and prick all over with a fork.
4. Press the remaining dough into the base of a lightly greased 23–24 cm (9–9½ inch) fluted loose-based flan tin or flan ring on a baking sheet. Prick evenly all over.
5. Bake the biscuits and base in a preheated moderate oven, with the biscuits on the lower shelf, allowing 15–20 minutes for the biscuits and 30–35 minutes for the base. Remove from the oven and leave to firm up then transfer to a wire rack and leave until cold.
5. Make the crème patissière: whisk the egg yolks with the sugar in a bowl, then beat in the flour, cornflour and a little of the milk, until smooth. Heat the remaining milk in a saucepan, pour on to the egg mixture and return to the pan. Cook gently, stirring continuously, until the mixture comes to the boil and thickens. Remove from the heat and beat in the vanilla essence and the butter. Cover and allow to cool.
6. If using fresh apricots, halve and remove the stones and put on a plate. Dredge lightly with caster sugar and leave to stand for 30 minutes or so.
7. To assemble: whip the cream until stiff and fold half into the crème patissière. Reserve 10 of the best apricot halves and slice the remainder, then fold into the cream mixture. Place the shortbread base on a serving plate and top with about two-thirds of the apricot cream. Cover with the meringue disc and spread the remaining apricot mixture in the centre.
8. Put the remaining whipped cream into a piping bag fitted with a vegetable star nozzle and pipe 10 large and 10 smaller whorls of cream evenly around the edge of the meringue. Top the small whorls with apricot halves and the larger one with shortbread biscuits. Decorate with pieces of angelica.

LEFT: Choc au rhum mousse RIGHT: Shortbread meringue gâteau

Choc au rhum mousse

Serves 8–10

350 g (12 oz) plain dark chocolate, broken into pieces	175 g (6 oz) caster sugar
	6 eggs, separated
2 tablespoons rum	150 ml (¼ pint) whipping cream
3 tablespoons water	ratafia biscuits or pieces of stem ginger, to decorate
175 g (6 oz) butter	

Preparation time: *about 30 minutes, plus setting overnight*
Cooking time: *about 5 minutes*

1. Put the chocolate in a heatproof bowl set over a saucepan of gently simmering water. Add the rum and water and heat gently until the chocolate melts, stirring until quite smooth. Allow to cool slightly.
2. Cream the butter and sugar together in a large bowl until very light and fluffy, then beat in the egg yolks one at a time.
3. Add the melted chocolate mixture and beat until light and fluffy.
4. Whisk the egg whites until stiff but not too dry and fold evenly through the chocolate mixture, using a large metal spoon.
5. Pour into a serving dish or 8–10 glasses and chill in the refrigerator overnight until set.
6. Decorate with whirls of whipped cream and ratafia biscuits or pieces of stem ginger.

Slimming Christmas

Jerusalem Soup

Turkey and Spinach Roulades

Red Fruit Salad with
Fluffy Yogurt

Jerusalem soup

Approx 50 calories per portion.

Serves 6	salt
1 large onion, peeled and chopped	freshly ground black pepper
1 kg (2 lb) Jerusalem artichokes, peeled and sliced	1 bay leaf
	1 blade mace
	1–2 tablespoons lemon juice
1.2 litres (2 pints) chicken stock	150 ml (¼ pint) milk
	chopped fresh parsley

Preparation time: *35 minutes*
Cooking time: *about 40 minutes*

1. Put the onion, artichokes and stock into a large saucepan with salt and pepper, the bay leaf and mace. Bring to the boil, cover and simmer for about 30 minutes or until very tender.
2. Discard the bay leaf and mace then purée the soup in a food processor or blender, or pass through a sieve.
3. Return to the rinsed-out pan with lemon juice to taste. [F] Bring to the boil, then add the milk, lower the heat and simmer for 2–3 minutes. Serve the soup in warmed individual soup bowls sprinkled with chopped parsley.

[F] Suitable to freeze for up to 3 months. Thaw overnight or reheat gently from frozen and continue with step 3.

Turkey and spinach roulades

Approx 210 calories per portion.

Serves 6	225g (8 oz) button mushrooms, thinly sliced
6 turkey fillets, 100–150 g (4–5 oz each)	grated rind of ½ lemon (optional)
salt	2 teaspoons cornflour
freshly ground black pepper	150 ml (¼ pint) plain unsweetened yogurt
ground coriander seeds	1 teaspoon French mustard
18–24 fresh spinach leaves, stalks removed	1 egg yolk
1 onion, peeled and very thinly sliced	TO GARNISH:
	parsley sprigs
450 ml (¾ pint) chicken stock	carrot and celery sticks

Preparation time: *about 30 minutes*
Cooking time: *1 ¼ hours*
Oven: *180°C, 350°F, Gas Mark 4*

1. Slit the fillets almost in half, then open out, lay flat between two sheets of cling film and beat out until thin. Season with salt, pepper and coriander.
2. Wash and dry the spinach leaves and lay over the turkey escalopes. Put a slice of onion in the middle and roll up the fillets; secure with wooden cocktail sticks.
3. Arrange the turkey roulades close together in a flame-proof casserole.
4. Bring the stock to the boil and season well with salt and pepper. Pour over the turkey roulades, add the remaining onion slices, cover and simmer gently for about 45 minutes or until tender. Alternatively cook in a moderate oven for ¾–1 hour.
5. Remove the turkey roulades, drain well and discard the cocktail sticks. Place on a serving dish and keep warm.
6. Return the cooking liquid to the boil and boil hard until reduced to just over 300 ml (½ pint). Strain into a clean saucepan and add the mushrooms and lemon rind.
7. Blend the cornflour with the yogurt, mustard and egg yolk and stir in a little of the sauce. Return to the saucepan and bring to the boil, stirring continuously. Simmer for 2–3 minutes, taste and adjust the seasoning and pour over the turkey roulades.
8. Garnish the turkey roulades with parsley sprigs and carrot and celery sticks. Serve with Brussels sprouts and French beans and, for those not on a diet, creamed potatoes or boiled rice.

CLOCKWISE FROM FRONT: *Turkey and spinach roulades, Red fruit salad, Jerusalem soup*

Red fruit salad

Approx 140 calories per portion.

Serves 6

1 × 425 g (15 oz) can black cherries, stoned and drained with juice reserved	225 g (8 oz) frozen raspberries
150 ml (¼ pint) apple juice	175 g (6 oz) black grapes, halved and seeded
450 g (1 lb) firm pears	TO SERVE:
	Fluffy yogurt (see below)

Preparation time: *15 minutes, plus soaking*
Cooking time: *5 minutes*

1. Place the cherries in a serving bowl. Put the cherry juice into a saucepan with the apple juice.

2. Peel, core and slice the pears and add to the pan. Bring to the boil and simmer for about 3–4 minutes. Add the contents of the pan to the cherries.

3. Sprinkle the still frozen raspberries over the warm fruit and leave at room temperature until thawed.

4. Finally add the grapes, mix well, and chill until required. Serve alone or with Fluffy yogurt.

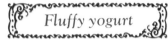

Fluffy yogurt

Turn a 150 ml (5 fl oz) carton natural yogurt into a bowl and stir with a fork until smooth. Whisk an egg white until very stiff and fold evenly through the yogurt. Sprinkle lightly with grated nutmeg and serve with the Red fruit salad.

Whisky steaks dijonnaise

Serves 6	2 tablespoons vegetable oil
6 fillet steaks	225 g (8 oz) button
salt	mushrooms, sliced
freshly ground black	5 tablespoons whisky
pepper	2 tablespoons herb mustard
1 clove garlic, peeled and	200 ml (7 fl oz) beef stock
crushed	watercress sprigs, to
50 g (2 oz) butter	garnish

Preparation time: *10 minutes*
Cooking time: *5–10 minutes*

1. Season the steaks on both sides with salt, pepper and garlic.
2. Heat the butter and oil in a large frying pan. Add the steaks and fry over a moderately high heat for 2–3 minutes on each side, to seal and brown. Fry for a further 1–3 minutes on each side, until the steaks are done to your liking. Remove from the pan and keep warm.
3. Add the mushrooms to the pan, fry for 1–2 minutes, then add the whisky, mustard and stock. Bring to the boil, stirring continuously, and season with salt and pepper. Return the steaks to the pan and turn to coat thoroughly in the sauce. Transfer to a warmed serving dish, pour over the sauce and garnish with watercress sprigs.
4. Serve at once with sauté potatoes or baked jacket potatoes, buttered carrots, French beans or mange-tout.

Traditional roast beef

Serves 8	50 g (2 oz) dripping
1.75–2.25 kg (4–5 lb)	YORKSHIRE PUDDINGS:
boned and rolled sirloin, rib	100 g (4 oz) plain flour
or topside joint of beef	2 eggs
salt	300 ml (½ pint) milk
freshly ground black	a little dripping
pepper	

Preparation time: *20 minutes*
Cooking time: *2–2 ½ hours*
Oven: *220°C, 400°F, Gas Mark 7*

1. Weigh the joint and calculate the cooking time at 20 minutes per 450 g (1 lb), plus 20 minutes for rare meat; 25 minutes per 450 g (1 lb) plus 25 minutes for medium meat; 30 minutes per 450 g (1 lb), plus 30 minutes for well-done meat.
2. Place the joint in a roasting tin with the thickest layer of fat uppermost. Season lightly with salt and pepper and spread with the dripping.
3. Roast in a preheated hot oven, basting several times, for the calculated time. Roast potatoes alongside the joint for the last 1½ hours of cooking.
4. Meanwhile make the Yorkshire puddings: sift the flour with a pinch of salt into a mixing bowl and make a well in the centre. Add the eggs and gradually beat in the milk to give a smooth batter.
5. Add a little dripping to 8 Yorkshire pudding tins or 16–18 patty tins and heat in the oven until piping hot. Pour the batter into the tins and bake below the joint for the last 25 minutes of cooking or until well puffed up and brown.
6. Transfer the joint to a warmed serving dish and surround with the roast potatoes and Yorkshire puddings. Serve with Brussels sprouts tossed in fried almonds or cauliflower in cheese sauce, with gravy made from the pan juices and horseradish sauce handed separately.

Traditional roast beef

Venison en croûte

Serves 8
2.25–2.75 kg (5–6 lb)
haunch of venison
175 g (6 oz) streaky bacon
rashers, rinded
salt
freshly ground black
pepper
4–5 tablespoons vegetable
oil or dripping
watercress sprigs, to
garnish
SAUCE:
3 tablespoons plain flour
450 ml (¾ pint) stock
(made from the bones or
from 1 beef stock cube)
4–5 tablespoons port
3 tablespoons redcurrant,
cranberry or bramble jelly
2–3 teaspoons lemon juice

STUFFING:
40 g (1½ oz) butter or
margarine
1 onion, peeled and
chopped
225 g (8 oz) mushrooms,
chopped
40 g (1½ oz) fresh white
breadcrumbs
1 teaspoon French mustard
¾ teaspoon dried basil
450 g (1 lb) puff pastry
(page 16)
beaten egg, to glaze

Preparation time: *about 1¼ hours*
Cooking time: *about 2¾ hours*
Oven: *200°C, 400°F, Gas Mark 6*
then: *220°C, 425°F, Gas Mark 7*
then: *180°C, 350°F, Gas Mark 4*

1. Bone the venison (ask the butcher to do this) and use the bones to make stock with 1.2 litres (2 pints) water. The boned joint should weigh about 1.75–2 kg (4–4½ lb).
2. Roll the venison into a neat joint, arrange the bacon rashers around it and tie in several places with string. Place the venison in a roasting tin, season well with salt and pepper and spread all over with dripping.
3. Roast the venison in a preheated hot oven for 1¼ hours, basting several times, then transfer to a plate and leave to cool completely.
4. Meanwhile make the sauce: skim any excess fat from the pan drippings. Stir the flour into the juices and cook, stirring for 1–2 minutes. Gradually stir in the stock and bring to the boil. Stir in the port, redcurrant jelly, lemon juice and salt and pepper to taste and stir over a gentle heat until the jelly dissolves. Strain the sauce into a saucepan, cover and cool.
5. Make the stuffing: melt the butter in a saucepan, add the onion and fry over a gentle heat until soft and lightly coloured. Add the mushrooms and fry for a further 1–2 minutes. Remove from the heat and stir in the breadcrumbs, mustard, basil and salt and pepper. Leave to cool.
6. When the venison is cold, remove the string. Roll out the pastry large enough to enclose the joint, reserving the trimmings. Spread the stuffing down the centre of the pastry and place the joint in the centre. Wrap up in the pastry, sealing the edges with water. Place seam side down in a lightly greased baking tin and brush all over with beaten egg. Re-roll the pastry trimmings and cut out pastry leaves. Decorate the pastry with the leaves and brush again with beaten egg.
7. Bake in a preheated hot oven for 30 minutes. Reduce the oven temperature and cook for 1 further hour, covering the pastry with a sheet of greaseproof paper when sufficiently browned.
8. Reheat the sauce and pour into a warmed sauce boat. Transfer the venison carefully to a serving dish and garnish with watercress sprigs. Serve in fairly thick slices with creamed potatoes or Parsnip duchesse potatoes (page 48) and spinach and buttered carrots, with the sauce handed separately.

Venison en croûte with Parsnip duchesse potatoes (page 48)

Roast stuffed leg of pork

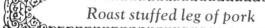

Serves 8–10

2.25–2.75 kg (5–6 lb) leg of pork joint, boned or rolled (ask the butcher to do this)

salt

freshly ground black pepper

vegetable oil

STUFFING:

225 g (8 oz) frozen chopped spinach, thawed

25 g (1 oz) butter or margarine

1 onion, peeled and finely chopped

2–3 rashers streaky bacon, rinded, boned and diced

1 pig's kidney, skinned, cored and chopped (optional)

50 g (2 oz) fresh white breadcrumbs

50 g (2 oz) shelled walnuts, roughly chopped

1 egg, beaten

Preparation time: *about 20 minutes*
Cooking time: *2½–3 hours*
Oven: *200°C, 400°F, Gas Mark 6*

1. Unroll the pork and season the inside with salt and pepper.
2. Drain the thawed spinach very thoroughly and place in a bowl.
3. Melt the butter in a frying pan, add the onion, bacon and kidney and fry over a gentle heat, stirring from time to time, for about 5 minutes or until lightly coloured. Add to the spinach with the breadcrumbs and walnuts, season with salt and pepper and stir in the egg to bind.
4. Spread the stuffing over the inside of the pork, re-roll and tie securely in places with fine string. Place the joint in a roasting tin, rub the skin all over with oil. Weigh the joint and calculate the cooking time at 30 minutes per 450 g (1 lb), and then sprinkle liberally with salt. Add a little more oil to the roasting tin.
5. Roast in a preheated hot oven for the calculated cooking time, basting once or twice. Roast potatoes alongside the joint for the last 1½ hours of cooking.
6. Serve the roast pork with roast potatoes, leeks in white sauce, apple sauce and gravy.

Baked gammon with ginger glaze

Serves 10–20

**2.25–3.5 kg (5–8 lb)
gammon joint either on the
bone or boned and rolled**

2 bay leaves

**2 tablespoons demerara
sugar**

150 ml (¼ pint) ginger ale

GLAZE:

**3 tablespoons ginger
marmalade**

**6 tablespoons demerara
sugar**

Preparation time: *5 minutes plus soaking time*
Cooking time: *2 hours 20 minutes – 3 hours 20 minutes*
Oven: *190°C, 375°F, Gas Mark 5*

Roast wild duck with orange and brandy sauce

1. Soak the gammon in cold water for 2–12 hours.
2. Drain the joint, then weigh and calculate the cooking time at 25 minutes per 450 g (1 lb), plus 20 minutes. For a joint over 2.5 kg (6 lb) allow 20 minutes per 450 g (1 lb), plus 20 minutes.
3. Place the joint in a large saucepan and pour in fresh cold water to cover. Add the bay leaves and sugar and bring to the boil. Cover, lower the heat and simmer for half the calculated cooking time.
4. Remove the joint from the pan and strip off the skin. Stand the joint on a sheet of foil in a roasting tin and score the fat diagonally in a trellis pattern. Mix together the marmalade and sugar and spread over the fat surface.
5. Pour the ginger ale around the joint and enclose in the foil, sealing the edges firmly. Cook in a preheated moderately hot oven for half the remaining cooking time.
6. Baste the joint with the ginger ale, rewrap in the foil and cook until 20 minutes before the end of the calculated time. Fold back the foil, baste again and return to the oven. Serve the gammon hot or cold.

Roast wild duck with orange and brandy sauce

4 oven-ready wild ducks
1 onion, peeled and roughly chopped
salt
freshly ground black pepper
40 g (1½ oz) butter or margarine
2 tablespoons vegetable oil
3 oranges
1 lemon
approx 150 ml (¼ pint) beef stock

1 tablespoon plain flour
150 ml (¼ pint) white wine
2 tablespoons redcurrant jelly
1–2 tablespoons thick honey
3–4 tablespoons brandy
TO GARNISH:
orange slices
parsley sprigs
trimmed spring onions

Preparation time: *30 minutes*
Cooking time: *about 1 hour*
Oven: *200°C, 400°F, Gas Mark 6*

1. Wipe the ducks inside and out and divide the onion between the cavities. Place the ducks in a large roasting tin, season well with salt and pepper and rub liberally with the butter. Add the oil to the tin.
2. Roast the ducks in a preheated hot oven for about 45 minutes, basting frequently, until tender and cooked through.
3. Meanwhile, pare the rind thinly from two of the oranges and cut into thin strips. Cover with cold water and cook for 8–10 minutes, until tender. Drain and reserve 150 ml (¼ pint) of the cooking liquid.
4. Squeeze the juice from all the oranges and the lemon and make up to 300 ml (½ pint) with the stock.
5. Transfer the ducks to a warmed serving plate and keep warm. Skim off the fat from the tin, leaving about 1 tablespoon and the pan juices. Sprinkle in the flour and cook for 1–2 minutes, stirring.
6. Gradually stir the orange cooking liquid, the stock mixture and the wine and bring to the boil. Stir in the redcurrant jelly, honey and salt and pepper and stir over a gentle heat until the jelly melts. Return to the boil and boil gently until reduced by about one-quarter.
7. Return the ducks to the tin, pour over the brandy and ignite. Baste two or three times with the sauce, then return the ducks to the serving dish and scatter over half the orange strips.
8. Pour the sauce into a warmed gravy boat and stir in the remaining orange strips.
9. Garnish the ducks with orange slices, parsley sprigs and spring onions. Serve with roast potatoes, Brussels sprouts and cauliflower, with the sauce handed separately.

Roast saddle of lamb

Serves 8
3–3.5 kg (7–8 lb) saddle of young lamb
1 garlic clove, peeled and cut
50 g (2 oz) butter or margarine, melted
salt
freshly ground black pepper
fresh rosemary sprigs

GRAVY:
25 g (1 oz) flour
450 ml (¾ pint) beef stock
2 tablespoons redcurrant jelly
3–4 tablespoons medium sherry
1 tablespoon tomato purée

Preparation time: *about 20 minutes*
Cooking time: *about 3–3½ hours*
Oven: 190°C, 375°F, Gas Mark 5

1. Weigh the lamb and calculate the cooking time at 25 minutes per 450 g (1 lb).
2. Rub the lamb all over with the cut side of the garlic clove, then brush all over with melted butter. Place the lamb in a large roasting tin, season with salt and pepper and lay the rosemary sprigs on top. Cover with a sheet of foil (do not tuck in).
3. Roast in a preheated moderately hot oven for the calculated time. Remove the foil after the first 30 minutes of cooking and baste occasionally.
4. Transfer the lamb to a serving plate, discard the rosemary and garnish with fresh rosemary sprigs; keep warm.
5. Make the gravy: strain off most of the fat from the pan leaving about 2 tablespoons including the juices. Stir in the flour and cook for 2–3 minutes, stirring, until it begins to brown. Gradually stir in the stock, redcurrant jelly, sherry and tomato purée. Bring to the boil, season well with salt and pepper and simmer for 2 minutes. Strain into a warmed gravy boat.
6. Serve the lamb with new potatoes, braised celery and buttered peas, accompanied by the gravy and extra redcurrant jelly.

Cakes

Glacé fruit cake

100 g (4 oz) glacé pineapple, chopped	225 g (8 oz) butter or margarine
150 g (6 oz) glacé cherries, washed, dried and chopped	150 g (6 oz) caster sugar
25 g (1 oz) crystallized ginger, chopped	3 eggs
	grated rind of 1 orange
25 g (1 oz) angelica, cut into narrow strips	grated rind of 1 lemon
50 g (2 oz) blanched almonds, chopped	3 tablespoons orange or lemon juice
100 g (4 oz) cut mixed peel	TOPPING:
225 g (8 oz) plain flour	3 tablespoons apricot jam, sieved
50 g (2 oz) cornflour	Brazil nuts
1 teaspoon baking powder	glacé cherries
½ teaspoon ground nutmeg	pecan nuts
	blanched almonds
	angelica strips

Preparation time: *about 30 minutes, plus cooling*
Cooking time: *2–2¼ hours*
Oven: *160°C, 325°F, Gas Mark 3*

This cake may be baked in a round or square tin or in a loaf tin. Allow about 15 minutes' longer baking time when using a loaf tin.

1. Grease and line with greased greaseproof paper a 20 cm (8 inch) round cake tin, or an 18 cm (7 inch) square tin, or a loaf tin about 24 × 14 × 7.5 cm (9½ × 5½ × 3 inches).
2. Mix together the pineapple, cherries, ginger, angelica, almonds, peel and 50 g (2 oz) flour. Sift remaining flour with the cornflour, baking powder and nutmeg.
3. In a mixing bowl cream the butter and sugar together until very light, fluffy and pale. Beat in the eggs one at a time, following each with a spoonful of the flour mixture.
4. Fold in the remaining flour, followed by the mixed fruit, orange and lemon rinds and juice.
5. Turn the mixture into the prepared tin and level the top. Bake in a preheated moderate oven for 2–2¼ hours or until the cake is firm to the touch and a skewer inserted into the centre comes out clean.
6. Cool in the tin for 10–15 minutes, then turn on to a wire rack. Brush the top of the cake while still warm with the apricot jam and then decorate attractively with Brazil nuts, almonds, pecan nuts, glacé cherries and angelica. Brush with more jam and leave to cool completely. If using a loaf tin turn out after 15 minutes and decorate the base of the cake. Store in an airtight container.

Madeira cake

225 g (8 oz) butter	100 g (4 oz) plain flour
225 g (8 oz) caster sugar	grated rind of 2 lemons
4 eggs	4 teaspoons lemon juice
225 g (8 oz) self-raising flour	piece of candied citron peel (optional)

Preparation time: *30 minutes, plus cooking*
Cooking time: *1¼–1½ hours*
Oven: *160°C, 325°F, Gas Mark 3*

This cake is an ideal alternative to a rich fruit Christmas cake. It will keep well for 2–3 weeks and may be covered with marzipan and royal icing like a normal Christmas cake. It is a good idea to dry the marzipan for only 2 days in a warmish atmosphere before adding the icing and to do this at the latest time possible before Christmas so that the cake is really fresh when cut.

1. Line a 20 cm (8 inch) round cake tin with greased greaseproof paper.
2. In a mixing bowl cream the butter and sugar together until very light, fluffy and pale. Sift the two flours together.
3. Beat the eggs into the creamed mixture following each addition with a spoonful of flour. Fold in the remaining flour, followed by the lemon rind and juice.
4. Turn the mixture into the prepared tin and if the cake is not to be iced lay 2 or 3 thin slices of citron peel on top. Bake in a preheated moderate oven for about 1¼–1½ hours or until the cake is well risen, firm to the touch and a golden brown, and a skewer inserted into the centre comes out clean.
5. Cool in the tin for 10 minutes then turn on to a wire rack and leave until completely cold. Carefully remove the lining paper and store in an airtight container. This cake will also freeze for up to 3 months.

LEFT TO RIGHT: Glacé fruit cake, Madeira cake, Chocolate layer cake

Chocolate layer cake

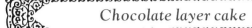

100 g (4 oz) butter or margarine	**CHOCOLATE ICING:**
100 g (4 oz) soft light brown sugar	3 tablespoons cocoa powder
100 g (4 oz) golden syrup	3 tablespoons hot water
175 g (6 oz) plain flour	100 g (4 oz) butter
65 g (2½ oz) cocoa powder, sifted	approx 225 g (8 oz) icing sugar, sifted
1 egg, beaten	1 tablespoon golden syrup
1 teaspoon bicarbonate of soda	a few drops of vanilla essence
150 ml (¼ pint) milk	chocolate curls (see below)

Preparation time: *40 minutes*
Cooking time: *20–25 minutes*
Oven: *180°C, 350°F, Gas Mark 4*

This is a dark Devil's Food-type cake with a lighter chocolate butter icing. It is possible to bake all three layers in the oven at the same time, with two tins on the upper shelf and one on the lower.

1. Grease and line three 20 cm (8 inch) sandwich tins with greased greaseproof paper.
2. Put the butter, sugar and syrup into a saucepan and heat gently until melted. Sift the flour and cocoa into a bowl, add the melted ingredients and mix until smooth and thoroughly blended.
3. Beat in the egg. Dissolve the soda in the milk, add to the mixture and beat very thoroughly.
4. Pour the mixture (it will be quite runny) into the prepared tins and bake in a preheated moderate oven for 15–20 minutes until just firm to the touch. Turn on to wire racks and leave to cool completely.
5. Make the icing: blend the cocoa with the hot water until smooth, then allow to cool. Beat the butter until soft, then gradually beat in the icing sugar alternately with the chocolate mixture. Add the syrup and vanilla essence. The mixture should be of a soft spreading consistency.
6. Put just under a quarter of the icing into a piping bag fitted with a large star nozzle. Use the remainder to sandwich the cakes together and spread on the top. Decorate the top with a round-bladed palette knife. Complete the decoration with a twisted piped edging just inside the edge of the cake. Sprinkle the centre with chocolate curls and leave to set.

Chocolate curls

A quick way to make these is to use a potato peeler to pare small curls off a block of plain dessert chocolate which is not too hard. For real curls, spread a thin layer of melted chocolate on a marble (or similar) slab, using a palette knife. Leave until just firm but not set hard, and then shave off curls, using a sharp, thin-bladed knife.

Light fruit cake

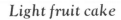

50 g (2 oz) glacé cherries, washed, dried and roughly chopped

175 g (6 oz) currants

175 g (6 oz) sultanas

50 g (2 oz) ground almonds

100 g (4 oz) cut mixed peel

225 g (8 oz) butter or soft margarine

225 g (8 oz) caster or soft light brown sugar

4 eggs, beaten

225 g (8 oz) plain flour

1 teaspoon mixed spice

½ teaspoon ground cinnamon

grated rind of 1 orange

2 tablespoons orange juice

2 tablespoons milk

Preparation time: *30 minutes, plus cooling*
Cooking time: *about 2 ½ hours*
Oven: *160°C, 325°F, Gas Mark 3*

Frosted coffee walnut cake, Nutfield cake

This is an economical fruit cake recipe which will keep for up to 3 weeks, but not for so long as a rich fruit cake. It may be covered with marzipan and royal icing and used as a Christmas cake or left plain for a cut and come again cake. If not to be iced, the cake may be sprinkled with demerara sugar or flaked almonds before baking.

1. Grease and line a 20 cm (8 inch) round cake tin with greased greaseproof paper. Mix the cherries, currants, sultanas, almonds and peel together in a bowl.
2. In a separate bowl cream the butter and sugar together until very light, fluffy and pale. Beat in the eggs one at a time, following each addition with a spoonful of the flour.
3. Sift the remaining flour with the spices and fold into the mixture with the orange rind, followed by the orange juice and milk. Finally add the dried fruit mixture.
4. Turn the mixture into the prepared tin and bake in a preheated moderate oven for about 2½ hours or until well risen and firm to the touch, and a skewer inserted in the centre comes out clean.
5. Leave to cool completely in the tin, then turn out, wrap in foil and store until required.

Nutfield cake

175 g (6 oz) butter or margarine

225 g (8 oz) caster sugar

4 eggs (size 1 or 2)

100 g (4 oz) ground almonds

75 g (3 oz) plain flour, sifted

a few drops of almond essence

ICING:

50 g (2 oz) plain dessert chocolate, broken into pieces

25 g (1 oz) butter

1 egg yolk

about 50 g (2 oz) icing sugar, sifted

a few toasted blanched almonds

Preparation time: *30 minutes, plus cooling*
Cooking time: *about 1 ¼ hours*
Oven: *180°C, 350°F, Gas Mark 4*

1. Grease and line a 20 cm (8 inch) round or 18 cm (7 inch) square cake tin with greaseproof paper.

2. In a mixing bowl cream the butter and sugar together until very light, fluffy and pale. Beat in the eggs one at a time, following each addition with 2 teaspoons of the ground almonds.

3. Fold the flour into the mixture with the remainder of the ground almonds and almond essence to taste.

4. Turn the mixture into the prepared tin and level the top. Bake in the centre of a preheated moderate oven for about 1¼ hours or until the cake is firm to the touch and golden brown, and a skewer inserted into the centre comes out clean.

5. Turn on to a wire rack and leave to cool completely.

6. Make the icing: put the chocolate and butter into the top of a double saucepan or a heatproof bowl set over a saucepan of gently simmering water. Heat until the chocolate is melted, then remove from the heat and beat until smooth.

7. Beat in the egg yolk and enough sugar to give a thick, smooth, spreading consistency. Cool slightly, then spread the icing over the top of the cake, swirl with a round-bladed knife and decorate with the toasted almonds.

Frosted coffee walnut cake

175 g (6 oz) butter or soft margarine

175 g (6 oz) caster or soft light brown sugar

3 eggs

175 g (6 oz) self-raising flour

2 tablespoons coffee essence or very strong black coffee

50 g (2 oz) shelled walnuts, chopped

FILLING:

50 g (2 oz) butter

100 g (4 oz) icing sugar, sifted

1 tablespoon coffee essence or very strong black coffee

FROSTING:

350 g (12 oz) caster sugar

2 egg whites

3 tablespoons water

1 tablespoon coffee essence or very strong black coffee

½ teaspoon cream of tartar

pinch of salt

walnut halves, to decorate

Preparation time: *about 45 minutes, plus cooling*
Cooking time: *about 40 minutes*
Oven: *190°C, 375°F, Gas Mark 5*

1. Grease and line the bases of two 20 cm (8 inch) sandwich tins with greased greaseproof paper, then dust lightly with flour.

2. In a bowl, cream the butter and sugar together until very light, fluffy and pale. Beat in the eggs one at a time, following each addition with a spoonful of the flour. Sift the remaining flour and fold into the mixture alternately with the coffee essence. Finally fold in the walnuts.

3. Divide the mixture equally between the sandwich tins and level the tops. Bake in a preheated moderately hot oven for 25–30 minutes or until well risen and just firm to the touch. Turn on to a wire rack and leave to cool completely.

4. Make the filling: beat the butter until soft, then beat in the icing sugar alternately with the coffee essence. Use to sandwich the cakes together.

6. Make the frosting: put all the ingredients into a heatproof bowl set over a saucepan of gently simmering water. Stir until the sugar is dissolved, then whisk with an electric hand whisk or balloon whisk, scraping down the sides of the bowl from time to time, until the mixture stands in peaks.

7. Spread the frosting over the whole of the cake, swirling with a round-bladed knife. Decorate with the walnut halves and leave to set.

Marzipan

Makes 450 g (1 lb)

100 g (4 oz) caster sugar

100 g (4 oz) icing sugar, sifted

225 g (8 oz) ground almonds

1 teaspoon lemon juice

few drops of almond essence

1 egg or 2 egg yolks, beaten

FOR THE GLAZE:

175 g (6 oz) apricot jam, warmed with 2–3 tablespoons water, then sieved

Preparation time: *about 10 minutes*

This quantity is sufficient to cover a 15 cm (6 inch) square or 18 cm (7 inch) round cake.

For an 18 cm (7 inch) square or 20 cm (8 inch) round you will require 550 g (1¼ lb) marzipan, using 125 g (5 oz) caster sugar, etc. For a 20 cm (8 inch) square or 23 cm (9 inch) round you will require 800 g (1¾ lb) marzipan, i.e. using 200 g (7 oz) caster sugar, etc.

1. Combine the sugars and ground almonds in a mixing bowl and make a well in the centre.
2. Add the lemon juice, almond essence and sufficient egg to mix to a firm but pliable dough.
3. Turn on to a lightly sugared board or work surface and knead until smooth. The marzipan can be wrapped in polythene or foil and stored for up to 2 days.

How to Marzipan a Cake
The same method is used for round and square cakes.

1. Place almost half of the marzipan on a surface dredged with icing sugar, or between two sheets of polythene or non-stick baking paper. Roll out evenly until a little larger than the top of the cake and cut out a round about 1 cm (½ inch) larger than the top of the cake. Set aside.
2. Roll out the remaining marzipan, including the trimmings, to a strip. Cut two lengths of string, one the circumference of the cake and the other the exact height of the cake. Using the string as a guide, cut the marzipan into strips the same width and circumference as the cake.
3. Stand the cake on a cake board. Brush the sides of the cake with the apricot glaze and fit the strips of marzipan around the cake. Press the ends together with a round-bladed knife.
4. Brush the top of the cake with the apricot glaze and position the circle of marzipan on top. Press the edges together with the round-bladed knife. If the marzipan is too moist rub lightly all over with sifted icing sugar.
5. Store the cake, uncovered, in a warmish place for at least 24 hours, and preferably a little longer, until dry. If the marzipan is still wet when the icing is added, the oils will seep into the icing and make unattractive stains.

Royal icing

To cover a 20 cm (8 inch) round or 18 cm (7 inch) square cake.

3 egg whites

about 675 g (1½ lb) icing sugar, sifted

2–3 teaspoons lemon juice, strained

1–1½ teaspoons glycerine (optional)

Preparation time: *about 15 minutes*

1. In a mixing bowl beat the egg whites until frothy, then gradually beat in half the icing sugar.
2. Add the lemon juice and glycerine and gradually beat in the remaining icing sugar, beating thoroughly after each addition to ensure a white icing, until the icing stands in soft peaks. Cover the bowl with a damp cloth or transfer to an airtight container and leave for 1–2 hours, to allow any air bubbles to come to the surface.

To Flat-ice a Cake with Royal Icing
1. Place the cake on a board, securing the base with a dab of icing. Stand on a turntable or up-turned plate. Put a quantity of icing in the centre of the cake and smooth out with a palette knife, using a paddling movement.
2. Draw an icing ruler or long palette knife carefully and evenly across the cake. Keep the ruler or knife at an angle of about 30°. Take care not to press heavily or unevenly.
3. Remove surplus icing by running the palette knife around the top of the cake, holding it at right angles.
4. If not sufficiently smooth, cover with a little more icing and draw the ruler across the cake again. Repeat until smooth. Leave to dry.
5. For a round cake: spread a thin but covering layer of icing all round the sides, again using a paddling action to push out as much air as possible.
6. Hold an icing comb or scraper or a palette knife at an angle of 45° to the cake and, starting at the back of the cake, slowly rotate the cake with your free hand, at the same time moving the comb slowly and evenly round the sides of the cake. Remove the comb fairly quickly at an angle, so that the join is hardly noticeable.
7. Lift any excess icing from the top of the cake with a palette knife, again rotating the cake. Leave to dry.
8. For a square cake: the best way of achieving even corners is to ice two opposite sides first and leave to dry before icing the other two sides. Spread some icing on one side, then draw the comb or palette knife towards you, keeping the cake still to give an even finish. Cut off the icing down the corner in a straight line and also off the top and base of the cake. Repeat with the opposite side and leave to dry. Repeat the process with the two remaining sides, and leave to dry.
9. Add a second layer of icing in the same way to the sides and top of the cake, making sure each layer is dry before adding the next.

Happy Christmas cake

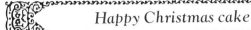

20 cm (8 inch) round fruit or madeira cake covered in marzipan	a little extra sifted icing sugar (optional)
1¼ recipe quantity royal icing (using 4 egg whites) (page 70)	14–16 royal icing Christmas roses (page 15)
about 1 teaspoon strained lemon juice	approx 24 marzipan holly leaves and berries (page 14)
yellow liquid food colouring	approx 10 marzipan ivy leaves (page 14)

Preparation time: *about 1½ hours, plus drying*

1. Attach the cake to a 25 cm (10 inch) round cake board with dabs of icing. Flat-ice the top of the cake, giving it two coats. Leave to dry.
2. Put 2 tablespoons icing in a piping bag fitted with a no. 2 writing nozzle. Draw one large and one small crescent shape (see picture) on a piece of stiff paper or card and cut out. Position on the cake and pipe an outline around the patterns, leaving just enough space to remove the patterns when dry. Keep the piping bag in a polythene bag.
3. Put 3 tablespoons icing in a bowl, adding enough lemon juice to give a flowing consistency. Put the icing into a paper icing bag without a nozzle, cut off the end and pipe the icing into the crescent shapes to fill them completely. Use a pin or cocktail stick to ease the icing into the corners and burst any air bubbles. Leave to dry.
4. Mark out and write 'Happy Christmas' in the space between the two crescents. Leave to dry.
5. Tint a tablespoon of icing yellow and put into a piping bag fitted with a no. 2 nozzle. Use to overpipe the 'Happy Christmas'.
6. With the white writing nozzle pipe a surround of small dots to each crescent shape.
7. Thicken the remaining icing a little with extra sifted icing sugar if necessary, until it stands in stiff peaks.
8. Spread fairly thickly all round the sides of the cake. Using a palette knife or spoon handle, pull the icing up into 'peaks' all round the sides and just up and over the top edge of the cake. Leave to dry.
9. Finally position the Christmas roses, ivy leaves, holly leaves and berries on the icing crescent (see picture). Attach them with a dab of icing and leave to dry.

Happy Christmas cake

Lattice Christmas cake

20 cm (8 inch) round fruit or madeira cake covered in marzipan and flat-iced

⅓ recipe quantity royal icing (using 1 egg white) (page 70)

holly berry red food colouring, powder or paste

approx 1 metre (1 yard) red ribbon 3–4 cm (1¼–1½ inches) wide

approx 1 metre (1 yard) green ribbon 1 cm (½ inch) wide

8–12 marzipan holly leaves and berries (page 14)

6–8 marzipan mistletoe leaves and berries (page 14)

5–7 moulded marzipan roses (page 15) or royal icing Christmas roses (page 15)

Preparation time: *about 2 hours, plus drying*

1. Make sure the flat-iced cake is quite dry before you start to decorate and that it is firmly attached with icing to a cake board approx 5 cm (2 inches) larger than the cake.
2. Mark a 10 cm (4 inch) square in the centre of the cake. Using a no. 2 plain writing nozzle and a piping bag half-filled with white royal icing, pipe straight lines over the two opposite sides of the square, from edge to edge of the cake. Fill in with straight lines so there are 5 or 7 lines between the first two lines and continue to fill the cake keeping the lines equidistant. Leave to dry.
3. Turn the cake round and add lines as before but at right angles to the first ones. Leave to dry.
4. Repeat by overpiping on top of the first lines so that they are all 2 layers deep and form a trellis. Leave to dry thoroughly.
5. Tint a small amount of the icing red with food colouring. Put into a piping bag fitted with a no. 2 writing nozzle. Overpipe lines across the cake to give a third layer to two sides of the square and then pipe over the alternate white lines in between. Turn the cake and repeat at right angles to complete the lattice. Leave to dry.
6. Fill a piping bag fitted with a star nozzle with white icing. Pipe a twisted loop edging around the top of the cake. Make 2 stars under every other loop on the side of the cake in graduated sizes.
7. Pipe large stars around the base of the cake to match the loops and pipe 2 stars above every alternate one as under the top edging so that they match. Leave to dry.
8. Tie red and green ribbons around the sides of the cake, finishing with a bow, if liked.
9. Decorate the top of the cake with 2 or 3 holly leaves and berries at each corner of the square and arrange roses or Christmas roses, rose leaves, mistletoe leaves and berries in the centre, attaching with a dab of icing.

This design can also be adapted to fit a square cake, by positioning the square in the centre of the cake.

Christmas tree cake

20 cm (8 inch) square fruit or madeira cake covered with marzipan and flat-iced with 2 coats

1 metre (1 yard) red or green ribbon 2.5 cm (1 inch) wide

⅓ recipe quantity royal icing using 1 egg white (page 70)

9 marzipan Christmas trees with red tubs (page 14)

silver balls

3 marzipan holly leaves and berries (page 70) (optional)

Preparation time: *about 1½ hours, plus drying*

1. Arrange the ribbon carefully over the cake as in the picture, attaching with pins and/or dabs of icing.
2. Half-fill with icing an icing bag fitted with a no. 2 writing nozzle. Pipe a straight line parallel to the ribbon as in the picture and continue to pipe lines at about 1 cm (½ inch) intervals to the edge of the cake. Repeat on the other side.
3. Turn the cake and pipe across the first lines parallel to the edge of the cake (not to the first lines) from the ribbon to the edge of the cake, piping two lines close together, then leave about 1 cm (½ inch) gap and pipe two more. Continue in this way as in the picture. Leave to dry.
4. Mark out the word 'NOËL' on the top of the cake between the ribbon and pipe a double row of icing over the letters. Leave to dry, then overpipe and dry again. Finally pipe a series of dots to cover the letters.
5. Fill a piping bag fitted with a large writing nozzle (no. 3 or 4) and pipe a twisted line or row of dots just inside the ribbon on the centre edge. Leave to dry.
6. Pipe a row of large dots around the top edge of the cake. In the centre of each side, pipe three graduated dots down the side of the cake with 2 graduated dots each side. Apart from the front side, pipe a series of these dots at each end of the cake sides (see picture).
7. Pipe a large row of dots or a twisted continuous line all round the base of the cake to attach to the board. Find the centre and pipe two and one dot above the edging to correspond with those coming from the top edge of the cake and work more at each end of the sides. Leave to set.
8. Finally attach the Christmas trees, two on each side and one on the top as in the picture, with a dab of icing, and then the holly leaves and berries, if using. Silver balls can be added to the Christmas trees at the tips of the branches with a dab of icing to represent baubles. Leave to dry.

FRONT: Christmas tree cake BACK: Lattice Christmas cake

Christmas Abroad

Stollen
(GERMANY)

Christmas tree cookies
(SCANDINAVIA)

25 g (1 oz) fresh yeast or
15 g (½ oz) dried yeast
2 tablespoons warm water
75 g (3 oz) caster sugar
pinch of salt
6 tablespoons warm milk
2 tablespoons rum
few drops almond essence
400 g (14 oz) plain flour
1 egg, beaten

150 g (5 oz) unsalted butter, softened
50 g (2 oz) raisins
50 g (2 oz) glacé cherries, chopped, washed and dried
50 g (2 oz) currants
25 g (1 oz) angelica, chopped
50 g (2 oz) cut mixed peel
40 g (1½ oz) flaked almonds
sifted icing sugar

Preparation time: *30 minutes, plus rising*
Cooking time: *about 45 minutes*
Oven: *190°C, 375°F, Gas Mark 5*

This is the famous German Christmas cake bread, quite delicious to eat. It is a slow riser because of the large amount of fruit but well worth the time it takes to make.

1. Blend the yeast in the water. If using dried yeast, add 1 teaspoon of the sugar and leave in a warm place until frothy. Dissolve 50 g (2 oz) sugar and the salt in the milk. Add the rum, essence and yeast liquid.
2. Sift the flour into a bowl, making a well in the centre. Add the yeast mixture, egg, 75 g (3 oz) softened butter cut into small pieces, and the fruits and nuts. Mix to a soft dough and knead for 10 minutes by hand, or 4–5 minutes in a large electric mixer fitted with a dough hook.
3. Replace the dough in the bowl, cover with oiled polythene or a damp cloth and put to rise in a warm place until doubled in size – about 2 hours.
4. Knock back the dough and knead until smooth, then roll out to a rectangle about 30 × 20 cm (12 × 8 inches).
5. Melt the remaining butter and brush liberally over the dough; then sprinkle with the remaining caster sugar. Fold one long side over just beyond the centre and then the other long side to overlap the first piece well. Press lightly together and slightly taper the ends.
6. Place on a greased baking sheet, brush with melted butter and leave in a warm place until almost doubled in size.
7. Bake in a preheated oven for about 45 minutes, until well risen and browned. Cool on a wire tray. Before serving dredge heavily with sifted icing sugar and serve cut into fairly thin slices.

Makes about 30
75 g (3 oz) black treacle
100 g (4 oz) butter or margarine
4 cardamom seeds
50 g (2 oz) caster sugar
2 tablespoons ground almonds
200 g (7 oz) plain flour
½ teaspoon bicarbonate of soda

½ teaspoon ground cinnamon
½ teaspoon ground ginger
1 egg yolk
GLACÉ ICING:
75 g (3 oz) icing sugar, sifted
about 1 tablespoon warm water

Preparation time: *20 minutes, plus chilling*
Cooking time: *about 25 minutes*
Oven: *190°C, 375°F, Gas Mark 5*

1. Melt the treacle and butter in a pan.
2. Split the cardamom seeds open and crush the kernels finely. Add to the melted mixture with the sugar and almonds.
3. Sift the flour, bicarbonate of soda and spices into the mixture, add the egg yolk and work together to form a smooth dough. Wrap in foil and chill for 20 minutes.
4. Roll the dough out thinly on a lightly floured surface or between two sheets of cling film to about 5 mm (¼ inch) thick. Using biscuit cutters, cut into shapes such as stars, Christmas trees, circles, diamonds etc. about 5–6 cm (2–2½ inches) in diameter.
5. Place on greased baking sheets and bake in a preheated oven for about 10–12 minutes or until just firm to the touch.
6. Immediately make a hole at the top of each biscuit with a skewer. When firm enough to move, transfer to a wire tray and leave until cold.
7. For the icing add sufficient water to the icing sugar to give a smooth spreading consistency. Place in a piping bag fitted with a small plain nozzle (size 2 or 3) and pipe a line around each biscuit about 5 mm (¼ inch) from the edge; alternatively pipe small stars. Leave to dry and store carefully in an airtight container.
8. Carefully thread a piece of wool or coloured string through the holes in the biscuits, tie firmly and hang on the Christmas tree. If they are to be eaten they must be removed from the tree after several hours, but they may be left there indefinitely for decoration.

TOP: Christmas tree cookies BOTTOM: Stollen

Bûche de Noël
(FRANCE)

4 eggs
100 g (4 oz) caster sugar
65 g (3½ oz) plain flour
15 g (½ oz) cocoa powder
25 g (1 oz) butter, melted and cooled
FILLING:
4 tablespoons double cream
1 tablespoon milk
1 × 250 g (8¾ oz) can sweetened chestnut spread

CRÈME AU BEURRE AU CHOCOLAT:
75 g (3 oz) caster sugar
4 tablespoons water
2 egg yolks
100–175 g (4–6 oz) unsalted butter
50 g (2 oz) plain chocolate, broken into pieces
sifted icing sugar
marzipan holly leaves and berries, to decorate (page 14)

Preparation time: *about 45 minutes*
Cooking time: *25–30 minutes*
Oven: *190°C, 375°F, Gas Mark 5*

1. Line a Swiss roll tin, 30 × 25 cm (12 × 10 in), with greased greaseproof paper. Put the eggs and sugar into a bowl and whisk until the mixture is very thick and pale and the whisk leaves a heavy trail when lifted.
2. Sift the flour and cocoa together twice and fold into the mixture, followed by the cooled runny butter.
3. Turn into the prepared tin making sure there is plenty of mixture in the corners. Bake in a preheated oven for about 15–20 minutes, or until just firm and springy to the touch.
4. Turn out on to a sheet of greaseproof or non-stick silicone paper dredged with caster sugar. Peel off the lining paper, trim off the edges of the cake with a sharp knife, then roll up the cake with the sugared paper inside. Cool on a wire tray.
5. Whip the cream and milk together until stiff, then fold into the chestnut spread.
6. Unroll the cake carefully, remove the paper and spread evenly with the chestnut mixture. Reroll carefully.
7. For the crème au beurre: place the sugar in a heavy-based pan with the water and heat gently until dissolved. Bring to the boil and boil steadily for 3–4 minutes to 110°C/225°F or until the syrup forms a thin thread.
8. Pour the syrup in a thin stream on to the egg yolks, whisking all the time. Continue to whisk until the mixture is thick and cold. Beat the butter until soft and gradually beat in the egg mixture.
9. Place the chocolate with 1 tablespoon water in a bowl over a pan of hot water and stir continuously until smooth and melted. Cool, then beat into the syrup mixture.
10. Coat the cake with the chocolate mixture; then mark attractively with the tines of a fork. Chill until set. Before serving, dredge lightly with icing sugar and decorate with holly berries and leaves.

Roast goose
(FRANCE)

Serves 6–8
1 oven-ready goose, about 3–4 kg (7–9 lb)
25 g (1 oz) butter or margarine
1 onion, peeled and finely chopped
goose livers, finely chopped
2 teaspoons dried sage
1–2 tablespoons freshly chopped parsley
salt
freshly ground black pepper

75 g (3 oz) fresh white breadcrumbs
1 egg, beaten
300 ml (½ pint) dry white wine
300 ml (½ pint) stock made with the goose giblets (or chicken stock)
2 teaspoons cornflour
little lemon juice (optional)
TO GARNISH:
button onions
carrot sticks
parsley sprigs

Preparation time: *30 minutes*
Cooking time: *about 2–2¾ hours*
Oven: *220°C, 426°F, Gas Mark 7 then 180°C, 350°F, Gas Mark 4*

1. If using a frozen goose make sure it is completely thawed – allow at least 24 hours at room temperature. Remove the giblets and any excess fat inside the cavity.
2. For the stuffing, melt the butter in a frying pan and fry the onion until soft. Add the livers and cook for a few minutes, stirring frequently until cooked through. Turn the mixture into a bowl, add the sage, parsley, salt and pepper and then breadcrumbs. Add sufficient beaten egg to give a softish stuffing.
3. Use this stuffing to stuff the neck end of the goose and fasten with a skewer. Truss the bird lightly and prick all over with a fork or large darning needle.
4. Place the goose in a roasting tin, on a wire tray. Combine the wine and stock and pour over the goose.
5. Roast in a preheated oven for 20 minutes then remove from the oven. Baste with the pan juices, then cover the goose with greaseproof paper. Reduce the temperature to moderate, then return the goose to the oven and roast, allowing 15 minutes per 450 g (1 lb). Baste again halfway through the cooking time and remove the paper for the last 20 minutes to allow the skin to brown.
6. Place the goose on a warmed serving dish and keep warm. Spoon off all the grease from the pan juices, using paper towels to mop it all up. Strain the juices into a pan, add the cornflour blended with a little cold water and stir over a medium heat until the sauce thickens.
7. Garnish the goose with onions, carrots and parsley. Serve with Peas à la française (peas tossed with fried chopped bacon and onion and strips of lettuce).

FRONT: Roast goose served with Peas à la française BACK: Bûche de Noël

Vasilopitta
(GREECE)

350 g (12 oz) plain flour	4 eggs (size 1 or 2)
1 tablespoon baking powder	250 ml (8 fl oz) orange juice (fresh or canned)
1 teaspoon ground nutmeg	grated rind of 1 large orange
225 g (8 oz) unsalted butter	
450 g (1 lb) caster sugar	flaked or blanched almonds

Preparation time: *30 minutes*
Cooking time: *50–60 minutes*
Oven: *180°C, 350°F, Gas Mark 4*

This is a New Year's Cake served at the stroke of midnight on New Year's Eve in Greece. St Basil is the patron saint of Greece so the cake is also named after him. It is usually much larger than this version and always has a lucky coin baked into it, although the ingredients do vary from family to family. When it is cut, a piece is offered to the Holy Mother and St Basil and the rest cut up for the assembled gathering. Any left over is supposed to be given to the poor on the following day. If the lucky coin is in the piece left for St Basil, then everyone should have a happy year, and if in the leftovers, then the poor will be more than excited. Wrap the coin in foil before placing it in the mixture.

1. Line a roasting tin approx 30 × 25 × 5 cm (12 × 10 × 2 inches) with greased greaseproof paper.
2. Sift the flour, baking powder and nutmeg together.
3. Cream the butter and sugar until very light and fluffy then beat in the eggs, one at a time, following each with a spoonful of flour; then beat in about one-third of the flour.
4. Gradually beat in the orange juice, alternating with the remaining flour and orange rind, until smooth and evenly blended. Drop in the coin.
5. Turn into the prepared tin and either sprinkle with flaked almonds or write the new year's date on top of the cake with blanched almonds.
6. Bake in a preheated oven for 50–60 minutes until golden brown and just firm to the touch. Turn out carefully on to a wire tray and leave to cool.
7. Serve cut into squares or diamonds.

Filhos de natal
(SPAIN)

Makes about 60	4 eggs
2 teaspoons dried yeast	3 tablespoons brandy
1 teaspoon caster sugar	oil for deep frying
3 tablespoons warm milk	clear honey
500 g (1 lb 2 oz) strong white flour	approx 50 g (2 oz) chopped toasted almonds or hazelnuts
1 teaspoon salt	

Preparation time: *40 minutes, plus rising*
Cooking time: *about 30 minutes*

These Christmas fritters from Spain are traditionally served dipped in honey. Here they are sprinkled with nuts for extra interest. They are best eaten fresh.

1. Dissolve the yeast and sugar in the milk and leave to stand in a warm place until frothy – about 20 minutes.
3. Sift the flour and salt into a bowl and make a well in the centre. Pour in the yeast liquid, beaten eggs and brandy and mix to a smooth, elastic dough.
3. Knead on a floured surface for 5 minutes by hand or for 2–3 minutes in a large electric mixer fitted with a dough hook. Replace the dough in the bowl, cover with greased polythene or a damp cloth and leave to rise in a warm place for about 2 hours, or until doubled in size.
4. Knock back the dough and knead until smooth. Roll out on a floured surface to about 5 mm (¼ inch) thick. Cut some of the dough into strips about 5 cm (2 inches) long and 1 cm (½ inch) wide. Cut others into strips 7.5–10 cm (3–4 inches) long and tie carefully into knots.
5. Heat the oil to about 190°C/375°F or until a cube of bread browns in 30 seconds, and fry the fritters a few at a time until golden brown, turning over when necessary. Remove with a slotted spoon and drain on paper towels.
6. Dip a wet brush in the honey and brush over the fritters, then sprinkle with the nuts. Serve hot, warm or cold.

LEFT TO RIGHT: Ao 'a' tea Roa, Filhos de natal, Vasilopitta

Ao 'a' tea Roa
(NEW ZEALAND)

Serves 6–8

THE PUDDING:

225 g (8 oz) plain flour

225 g (8 oz) soft brown sugar

175 g (6 oz) sultanas

350 g (12 oz) raisins

50 g (2 oz) cut mixed peel

grated rind of 1 lemon

½ teaspoon mixed spice

100 g (4 oz) softened butter

2 teaspoons bicarbonate of soda

350 ml (12 fl oz) boiling water

2 eggs, beaten

LONG WHITE CLOUD:

1 × 425 g (15 oz) can apricot halves

¼ teaspoon ground cinnamon

1 litre (2 pint) carton or large block vanilla ice cream

2–3 tablespoons brandy

Preparation time: *30 minutes, plus soaking and chilling*
Cooking time: *3 hours*

The Maori name for this Christmas pudding, Ao 'a' tea Roa, describes the long white cloud which is always visible over the islands of New Zealand as you fly in. Roast turkey is traditionally served on Christmas Day followed by this pudding, which is light and airy, very suitable for their warm sunny Christmas weather.

1. Sift the flour into a bowl, add the sugar, dried fruits, peel, lemon rind and spice and mix well. Cut the butter into small pieces and dot over the mixture.

2. Dissolve the bicarbonate of soda in the water and pour over the mixture. Mix lightly, cover with a cloth and leave to stand overnight.

3. Next day add the beaten eggs and mix thoroughly. Turn into a greased 1.7 litre (3 pint) or two 900 ml (1½ pint) pudding basins. Cover with greased greaseproof paper (giving room for expansion) and then foil or a pudding cloth, and tie securely with string. Place in a large pan (or pans) of boiling water, so that the water comes halfway up the basins, and simmer for 3 hours, topping up the water as necessary.

4. Line a freezer tray or other container approx 30 × 10 cm (10 × 4 inches) with double foil and grease well. Remove the warm Christmas pudding from the basin and pack it into the tin, making it about 4 cm (1½ inches) thick. Chill until required.

5. Purée the apricots with some of the juice and flavour with the cinnamon.

6. To serve: unmould the pudding on a warmed long serving dish. Put slices or scoops of ice cream along the top of the pudding and coat with the apricot sauce. At the table, pour warmed brandy around the pudding on the warmed dish and set alight. Serve at once.

INDEX